Chess!

Chess!

A Fun Game to Learn and Play

A Chess Book

For Students and Adult Learners of Chess

Sinclair L. Wilkinson

Library of Congress Control Number: 2008902750
ISBN: Hardcover   978-1-4363-3036-7
                     Softcover   978-1-4363-3035-0

This book was printed in the United States of America.

To order additional copies of this book, contact:
Xlibris Corporation
1-888-795-4274
www.Xlibris.com
Orders@Xlibris.com
47743

CONTENTS

Chapter 1

1.0 What is Chess?... 19

1.1 The Correct Position of the Chessboard.......................... 20

1.2 Examine Chessboard... 21

1.3 Identifying the Pieces.. 22

Chapter 2

2.0 Chess Background... 25

2.1 A Brief History of Chess 25

2.2 The Main Objective of Each Chess Player 27

Chapter 3

3.0 Brief History of the Pawns.. 29

3.1 How to move the pawns 31

3.2 Summary Questions About the Pawns 36

3.3 What to Remember About the Pawns: 37

3.4 Brief History of the Knight 39

3.5 How to Move the Knight... 40

3.6 How to Capture a Piece with the Knight...................... 42

3.7 Summary Questions about the Knight.......................... 43

Chapter 4

4.0 Brief History of the Bishop 47

4.1 How to Move the Bishop... 48

4.2 Summary Questions about the Bishop.......................... 51

4.3 Brief History of the Rook 53

4.4 How to Move the Rook 54

4.5 Summary questions about the Rook 58

4.6 Brief History of the Queen 60

4.7 How to Move the Queen 62

4.8 Summary Questions about the Queen 65

Chapter 5

5.0 Brief History of the King 68

5.1 How to move the King 69

5.2 Special King Move—Castling 71

5.3 Summary Questions about the King 76

5.4 Understanding the value of the pieces 80

5.5 Exchanging of pieces/Best Choices: 80

5.6 Summary Questions on Correct Exchanges 83

Chapter 6

6.0 Who Should Play First? 86

6.1 Review 87

6.2 Answers to the Previous Questions 90

Chapter 7

7.0 Chess Symbols 92

7.1 Algebraic Notation 93

7.2 Writing Castle moves: 97

7.3 What is a Check? 100

7.4 What is Checkmate? 100

7.5 What is a Stalemate? 105

7.6 Forms of Draws 108

Chapter 8

8.0   Opening Moves..110

     Giuoco Piano...111

     Sicilian Defence...112

     The English Opening 113

     The Caro-Kann Defence 114

     The French Defence 115

     King's Gambit..116

8.1   Important Opening Tips:..117

Chapter 9

9.0   Middle-Game Advantages 118

9.1   Chess Tactics 121

9.2   Different Types of Fork 121

9.3   The Pin...128

9.4   Breaking the Pin..132

9.5   Discovered Check...135

9.6   What is a Decoy? 137

9.7   What is an Overload? 141

9.8   What is a Deflection?..145

9.9   Summary questions 148

Chapter 10

10.0 Double Check 152

10.1 The Skewer 155

10.2 Removing the Guard 158

10.3 Offering A Draw 160

10.4 How to Force a Draw..162

Chapter 11

11.0 How Best to Open 167

11.1 Using the Clock 168

11.2 Summary Questions: 169

11.3 Answers to Questions 171

Chapter 12

12.0 Chess Etiquette 174

Chapter 13

13.0 Defense against Checkmate 180

13.1 Visualizing Checkmate 182

13.2 Combinations 186

13.3 Your End Game 192

Chapter 14

14.0 Scenarios: Preparing for Checkmate............................. 203

Chapter 15

15.0 Important Chess Terms 247

Chapter 16

16.0 World Chess Champions 254

16.1 Answers to Scenarios Questions 1-60 262

Acknowledgement

To my chess mentor:

To Mr. Adolph Potter, a native Virgin Islander, who has been my chess mentor, advisor, and friend since the 1970s.

Originally, I met Mr. Adolph Potter in 1975 during a local chess tournament in St. Thomas, US Virgin Islands. At that time, I was just learning the basic fundamentals of chess and was rather fascinated to meet someone who represented the US Virgin Islands in several World Chess Olympiads in Switzerland, Germany, France, Guatemala, Costa Rica, and Mexico.

After that chess tournament ended, I was amazed with Mr. Potter's willingness to sit with me and other chess enthusiasts to share his knowledge, passion, and experience of the game.

Since then, Mr. Potter spent countless hours with me playing, analyzing, and reviewing hundreds of opening, middle, and end games. He has enlightened my chess horizons with his wisdom and passion for the game. Consequently, his teaching has led me to win in many local chess tournaments. I have become a chess instructor and a participant in three World Chess Olympiads: Bled, Slovenia; Mallorca, Spain; and Torino, Italy. I was also selected to represent the Virgin Islands in the 2008 World Chess Olympiad in Germany.

It is often said that if you have played chess on the island of St. Thomas, US Virgin Islands, you must have played chess with Mr. Adolph Potter. Many students and competitive chess players in the U.S Virgin Islands have benefited from his tutelage. We all owe a debt of gratitude to this chess teacher.

I would like to encourage all students of chess to acquire the values and benefits of this wonderful game. We can become mentors to those who are eager to learn. We must also continue to honor the enduring spirit of those who have kept chess in our hearts and minds. I applaud Mr. Adolph Potter who continues to be an inspiration to all chess players on St. Thomas, US Virgin Islands.

Other Acknowledgements

My Family:
Emily Wilkinson—Mother
Marlene Wilkinson—Wife

Children
Kobie, Kurt, Matthew, Jason, Gabriel

Our Chess Club Members:
Allen, Frank, Bob, Herman, Glen, and Dennis

Youth and future masters:
Sherwin, Benjamin, Nathan, Briana, Jamari, Zhyd, and Precious.

All of the coaches and students in the
Virgin Islands Learning Institute Chess program
especially Karen.

To my friend C. Sarauw

Artist: Meldon Warner

Editor: Dr. George Newton
Advisor: Adolph Potter

Introduction

I have taught and tutored chess to hundreds of youngsters, teenagers, and adults over the past twenty-five years. Throughout these years, I met and encouraged young people and adults who were interested in learning and playing chess to play the game. Often, these first-time enthusiasts would ask some basic but interesting questions: How do I move chess pieces? How do I set up a chessboard? When and where chess started? How did chess expand throughout the world? What are some of the basic principles and etiquette of the game? Who are some of the present and past champions? How may I end a chess game?

Although I was familiar with the responses as I tapped my own experiences, I still researched these questions. Of course, some required more in-depth answers, and I tried to address other related concerns with pertinent information.

Over the years, I realize that much work is required to provide simple and basic chess information to all who were interested. I also saw the need for chess teachers and players to introduce and expose chess to our students and our adult population. Further, I felt that someone in our islands had to initiate the move and present this "game of life" to everyone. It is this emotion and spirit that has motivated me to write this book.

The book is divided into different sections. An effort is made in the first few chapters to describe the game of chess, explain how to position the board, examine the history of each piece, demonstrate the movement of each piece, and provide some practical scenarios and questions for each reader. In the second half, a more in-depth analysis of the game is presented. I focused on terms and meanings, information about world chess leaders, pins and forks, stalemates, how to force draws, and scenarios showing how to checkmate an opponent in one or two moves.

I hope that the information presented would benefit chess enthusiasts.

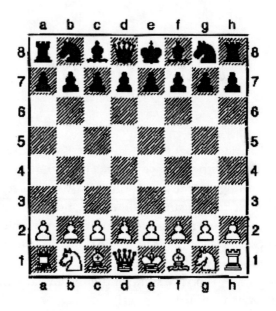

Goal

To promote the educational, historical, social, and cultural significance of chess among our youth, adult learners, and others in the wider community.

Objectives:

The learner of chess will be able to:

1. Identify each minor and major chess piece
2. Demonstrate how each piece moves, advances and captures
3. Explain the historical development of chess
4. Identify some of the places in the world where chess is very popular
5. Identify some of the past and present world chess champions
6. Solve a number of chessboard scenarios in one or two moves
7. Analyze and develop personal offensive and defensive tactical strategies
8. Use algebraic notations to record various chess games
9. Give the correct meanings to important chess terms
10. Visualize positional advantages and checkmates

Chapter 1

What is Chess?

Chess is an abstract strategy board game that is played by two players. This game is played on a square board that consists of rows called *ranks,* these are the squares that travel in a horizontal direction or from east to west, and *files,* the squares that are moving in a vertical direction or from north to south. The entire board consists of sixty-four squares of alternative colors of light and dark: eight vertical rows and eight horizontal rows. Each row consists of eight squares.

When a player is setting up a chessboard, it must be positioned so that a light square, usually white, is placed on the extreme lower right-hand side, designated as **h1**, and a black square must be placed on the lower left-hand corner, designated as **a1**. It is important to note that some chessboards are built without numbers or letters, but all boards should be turned in the same legal position when a game is being played. The black square must be placed on a lower left corner, and a white square must be placed on the lower right corner.

Let us look closely at how a chessboard should be placed when one is starting a game. Notice that there are a number of horizontal squares that are numbered from 1 to 8, these are called *ranks,* and some vertical squares that are marked with the letters moving from a to h, these are called *files.* For clarification, it is acceptable to say the first, second, third, or fourth rank or the **a**, **b**, **c**, or **d** file.

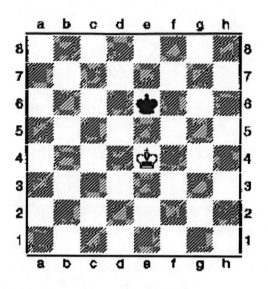

The Correct Position of the Chessboard

When a chessboard is officially set up, there are a number of objects or pieces on both side of the chessboard. These pieces are colored either white or black. If one notices closely, many of these pieces look alike. There are a total of thirty-two pieces. Of these pieces, some look like horses. Others have pointed heads. Crowns are placed on the heads of two pieces. Two pieces stand with crosses on their heads and are standing taller than all the other pieces on the board. Lastly, sixteen smaller pieces are similarly shaped.

When the chessboard is closely examined, one can also notice some lines that are running diagonally. These lines are touching the northeast, southwest, northwest, and southeast corners of the board. Each row consists of different numbers of squares because the length of each diagonal line is different.

FIDE: Article 2.4

The eight vertical columns of squares are called "files." The eight horizontal rows of squares are called "ranks." A straight line of squares of the same color, touching corner to corner, is called a "diagonal."

When a chessboard is positioned in front of two chess players, it must be placed flat. Observe the colors of the squares at the bottom right—and left-hand corners.

For the side that consists of *the black* pieces, the *white square* on the right-hand side would be identified as **a8**, and the black square on the left hand side would be identified as **h8**.

The first few questions one may ask are:

1.   What is the name of each piece on the chessboard?
2.   On which squares should the pieces be placed?
3.   How to move the pieces?
4.   How to determine who plays what color?
5.   Where and when this game begins?
6.   Why is this game so popular around the world?
7.   How did this game spread to so many countries?

Examine the details of the chessboard below

Let us look at the above chessboard. Notice that there are eight vertical and eight horizontal lines. Also notice the white and black diagonal lines. Notice the squares that are marked **a** to **h** and those squares that are numbered **1** to **8**.

Let us identify some of these squares:

A.   Identify the square that is marked **a1**.
B.   Identify the square that is marked **h8**.
C.   Identify the square that is marked **f5**.

D. Identify the square that is marked **b7**.
E. Identify the square that is marked **h1**.
F. Identify the square that is marked **c4**.
G. Identify the square that is marked **h3**.
H. Identify the square that is marked **e5**.

Identifying the Pieces

The smallest pieces on the board are called *pawns*. These pawns stand on the second and the seventh ranks. There are eight white and eight black pawns. Some people sometime refer to the pawn as the "heart and soul" of a chess game. Further details about the pawns will be discussed in a later chapter.

Let us identify another piece—the rooks.

On the squares that are marked **h1, h8, a1,** and **a8** sit four large pieces. These pieces are called *rooks*. There are a total of four rooks: two black rooks and two white rooks. Further details about the importance and the value of these rooks will be presented later. Other pieces that are shaped like horses are the *knights*.

Standing next to the rook are pieces that look like horses. These pieces are called *knights*. The starting squares for the knights are **b1, g1, b8,** and **g8**. There are a total of four knights, two black knights and two white knights. The value and the importance of the knights will be discussed later.

The pointed pieces are called the *bishops*.

Standing next to the knights are four straight pieces with some pointed tips. These pieces are called *bishops*. The bishops sit on the c1, f1, c8 and f8 squares. There are a total of four bishops: two black and two white bishops. The specific moves and the value of these pieces will be presented in a further chapter.

The pieces with the crowns are called the *queens*.

Standing next to the bishops, on the right side (if you are viewing the board from the white or the **a1** side) and on the left side of the bishop (if your are viewing the board from the black or the **a8** side), are two pieces with crowns on their heads. These two pieces are called *queens*. One piece stands on the **d1** square and the other stands on the **d8** square.

At the beginning of a game, only two queens are placed on the board. During the game, other queens can appear after pawns are promoted to the eight or the first ranks. Further details about how this can be achieved will be discussed in a later chapter.

The tallest pieces on the board are the *kings*.

Standing next to the queens are the two tallest pieces on the chessboard. One is colored black and the other is white. These pieces are called *kings*. There are only two kings. The kings stand on the **e1** and **e8** squares. Further details about these important pieces will be presented later.

Chapter 2

Chess Background

Now that we were introduced to the chessboard and the pieces, it is important to give a brief overview of the game. Let us explore the history of chess. We will look at how chess was developed, its present status, and what the future holds for this most popular and beautiful game.

A Brief History of Chess

The Past

Chess is one of the oldest games. Unfortunately, nobody really knows just how old. Some people claim that chess is more than two thousand years old. However, the game is thought to have originated in northern India or Afghanistan around 600 AD. There are also some evidence that a version of chess, *xiangqi*, existed in China hundreds of years earlier. Coincidentally, this type of Chinese chess was somewhat related to Western chess. Its rules, board configuration, piece movements, and strategies have proven to be the logical precursor to our modern chess.

Another version of chess that closely resemble the game that we now play in the western world started in India around 600 AD. From India, chess began to spread to different parts of the world. In the fifteenth century, chess evolved to closely resemble the game we now play.

The growth of chess really started blossomed in the 1800s when organized tournaments chess clubs, championship games, and titles like Masters, International Masters, Grandmasters, and ratings were introduced.

The first international chess tournament was played London in 1851. This tournament was won by a German, Adolf Anderssen. The first great

American-born player was Paul Murphy who was of Irish ancestry. He was one of the world's best players in the 1850s. In modern times, Bobby Fischer became the US Champion at the age of fourteen. He is the first native-born US citizen to hold the title of World Chess Champion. There have been a number of great world champions such as the great Jose Capablanca from Cuba, Mikhail Tal, Alexander Alekhine Anatoly Karpov, and a host of other great Russian players. Also, there were Machgielis Euwe from Holland and most recently Viswanathan Anand from India.

The Present

Chess has grown, and it is now the most popular game in the world. There are hundreds of millions of players who are involved in thousands of clubs around the planet. These players are actively promoting chess in different schools, online sites, neighborhood clubs, community tournaments, and chess federations.

Chess is growing immensely among children in schools, and many parents have recognized the social and intellectual benefits that are associated with the game. Chess tournaments for adults and youth are held in many countries. With the computer, a chess player can now contact players from any part of the world. This technical resource has enabled the skill levels of chess players to improve by leaps and bounds. Women and girls are learning chess in record numbers especially in many undeveloped countries.

The Future

Chess is the fastest growing sport in the world, and much future growth is anticipated. Younger players, especially girls, are achieving grandmaster status. Future players will have to move more accurately in their openings as computer training becomes available to more people.

Many more school clubs will connect with other school clubs in different districts all around the world. Tournaments will be played online by these clubs, and students will receive official ratings based on their game performances. Through this medium, the world of chess will become smaller and better connected. Players will become more acquainted with different societies and cultures, professional coaches will be able to reach more people, more nations will host international tournaments.

The main objective of each chess player

The main objective of any player in a game is to apply the rule of the game and ultimately win.

FIDE is the international body that governs international chess tournaments. One of their governing rules (Article 1:2) states that the objective of each player who is engaged in the game of chess, is to place the opponent's king "under attack" in such a way that the opponent would have no legal move. The rule further states that the player who achieves this goal is said to have "checkmated" the opponent's king and that player would have won the game.

Each of the chess pieces on the chessboard moves differently. Each may be moved to another position or may capture an opponent's piece by applying the rules that govern the movement of that specific piece. This is done by landing on the appropriate square with the moving piece and removing the defending piece from that square.

FIDE: Article 3.1

It is not permitted to move a piece to a square occupied by a piece of the same color. If a piece moves to a square occupied by an opponent's piece, the latter is captured and removed from the chessboard as part of the same move.

Chapter 3

How to move the chess pieces

    A. The Pawns
    B. The Knights
    C. The Bishops
    D. The Rooks
    E. The Queens
    D. The Kings

THE PAWN

 A pawn has a value of 1 point

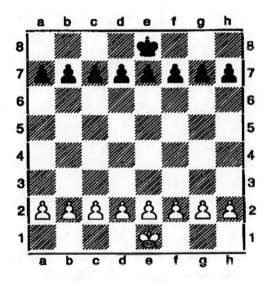

Brief History of the Pawns

Many people look at pawns as the least valued member of a royal family. In earlier years, these pawns were the foot soldiers who were committed to protect the king from expected attacks.

To many people, the pawns seem to be unimportant because they only value one point each. Yes, pawns are the least valued pieces among all the other pieces.

However, if these pawns progress and reach the eighth or first ranks, they can be promoted and become the most valuable pieces on the chessboard.

There are a total of sixteen pawns: eight white pawns and eight dark pawns. A pawn can only move one or two squares forward, or vertically, from their starting squares. Pawns never capture or move backward.

Pawns cannot jump over other pieces. They are the only pieces that capture differently than how they move. Pawns move *vertically* and capture *diagonally*.

Years ago, pawns represented foot soldiers. These foot soldiers carried shields to protect themselves and spears to stab their enemies. Since the shields were held in front of them, they could not attack their enemies straight on with their weapons. Their enemies were speared diagonally from the sides of their protected shields.

During the Middle Ages, monks tried to represent the pawns as citizens. The first pawn on **a2** was an agricultural worker, the second a farrier, the third a weaver, the fourth a businessman, the fifth a doctor, the sixth an innkeeper, the seventh a policeman, and the eighth a gambler. These differences are no longer used in modern-day chess.

Pawns were fully aware of their rights, duties, and responsibilities. Some were captured while making an effort to protect their king, and others became full members of the royal family. Pawns were acutely aware of their responsibilities. They know that if they dedicate themselves as fighters, work hard and smart, work together, escape planned traps, they all would be rewarded at the end of a battle.

When we play our modern-day chess, we promote pawns to queens, rooks, knights, or bishops when they advance to the first or eighth rank. When a pawn reaches the eighth or first rank and a queen is attained, that movement is called *queening* or *promotion*. If one chooses to take a knight, bishop, or rook instead, that movement and selection is called *underpromotion*. It is important to note that a player can have as many as nine queens if these pawns do reach the back ranks. A player does not need all nine queens to checkmate an opponent king.

The role and duty of a pawn is a good life's lesson for all students. Pawns have proven that it is not how one starts out in life, but the kind of success one can achieve through hard work, respect, good attitude, determination, and loyalty. Pawns have proven that if people perform little tasks well, they will accomplish much in the end. Pawns have demonstrated that if people of lower-level status organize themselves and work together, their collective energies will have more impact than individuals working alone. Pawns believe that in unity, there is strength.

How to move the pawns

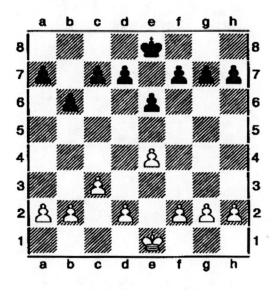

All white pawns start on the second rank. The black pawns start on the seventh rank. When a game starts, a white pawn can move one or two squares on the first move. For example, the pawn on the white side that starts on **e2,** can move to **e3** or **e4.** On the black side, a pawn that starts on **e7** can move to **e6** or **e5.** After a pawn advances one or two squares on its first move, it cannot move two squares on any other move.

Also, all pawns advance vertically, but must move diagonally to capture an opponent piece. Again, when a pawn reaches the eighth or the first rank, a player can exchange that promotional pawn for any desired piece. That player can ask for a queen, rook, knight, or bishop. It is not legal to ask for another king or another pawn.

Again, all pawns start on the second and seventh ranks. Any pawn, at any time, can move *one or two squares* on the first move as long as that pawn is not being impeded by another piece.

Notice on the previous chessboard that the white pawns are on the **e4** and the **c3** squares. Notice also that black has moved to the **e6** and the **b6** vertical lines. Both of these moves for white and black are acceptable or legal moves.

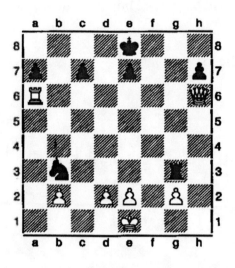

On the above board above, the **b2** *cannot* capture the knight on the **b3** square. The white pawn on the **g2** square *cannot* capture the rook on the **g3** square.

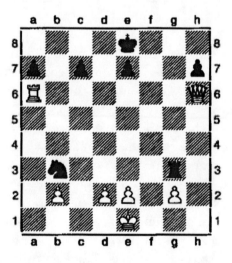

On the black side, the pawn that sits on the **h7** square *cannot* capture the queen that sits on the **h6** square. Also, the pawn that sits on the **a7** square *cannot* capture the rook that sits on the **a6** square.

The white pawns cannot eat any of the above advancing black pieces, and the black pawns cannot capture any of the larger advancing white pieces.

It is also important to note that the white and black pawns cannot jump over any of these advancing pieces.

The white or black pawns can advance or move forward once the vertical file is clear. If, however, a piece is positioned in the square directly in front of a given pawn, that pawn cannot advance. Look at the examples on the chessboard on the above page again. Neither the **g2** nor the **b2** pawns for white can advance. The other white pawns can. For the black, neither the **h7** nor the **a7** pawns can advance. The remaining pawns can because the vertical files in front of them are clear.

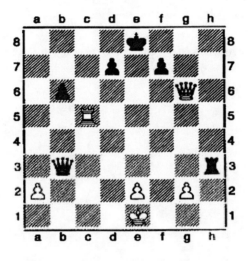

Notice on the above board that the white pawns on the **a2** and the **g2** squares can eat any of the black pieces. The **g2** pawn can capture the black rook that sits on the **h3** square, and the **a2** pawn can capture the black queen that sits on the **b3** square.

On the black side, the **f7** pawn can capture the white queen that sits on the **g6** square, and the **b6** pawn can capture the rook that sits on the **c5** square.

Remember, pawns move vertically and capture pieces diagonally. The white pawn that captures the rook will move from the **g2** square to the **h3** square. The pawn that captures the queen will move from the **a2** square to the **b3** square. On the black side, the black pawn would move from the **f7** square and move the **g6** square after the capture, and the pawn on the **b6** square would move the **c5** square after the capture.

It is important to note that pawns cannot move backward. They can only move forward and capture diagonally.

What is En Passant

Among a few of the special moves that one can make in the game of chess is a move that is called *en passant*.

This special move does not happen too often in a chess game, but it is important to be knowledgeable of this important move. En passant is a French word that means "in passing." This move only involves the pawns. If a white pawn is on the fifth rank, and your opponent advances a pawn two squares vertically, denying you the capture, you can capture that pawn, and move the white pawn on that denied diagonal square on the sixth rank.

Look at an example on the board below. The white pawn on **a5** can capture the black pawn that is on **b5** because the **b5** pawn has "bypassed" the **b6** square where the white pawn could have made a capture. After this capture is made, the white pawn will then be placed on **b6**. This capture opportunity can only be made once for that move, and it must be done immediately after the opposing pawn advances to those two squares.

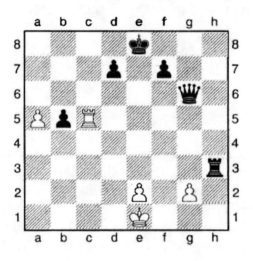

Let us look at another example on the board below. If the pawn that sits on **d7** moves directly to **d5**, it is denying the white pawn from capturing it. The white pawn *can, but not necessarily have to,* capture the black. The white pawn will, after the capture is made, advance to the **d6** square.

These special moves can only be done on the sixth rank for white and on the third rank for black. Look at the other examples that are listed below. Examine how the black conducts an *en passant* move.

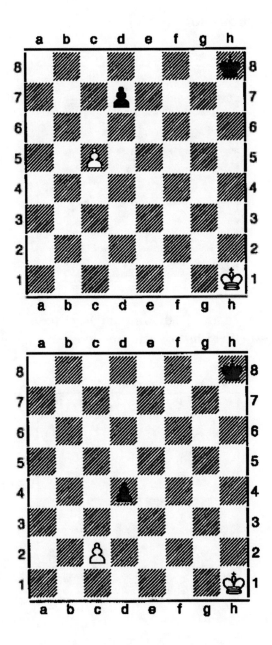

On the previous board, note that if the white pawn on **c2** advances to **c4,** the black pawn that sits on **d4** can capture the white pawn and advance to the **c3** square.

Summary Questions about the pawns

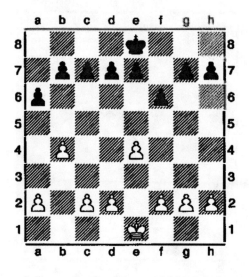

Look at the board above. Both white and black have made their first two moves. Indicate whether white or black moves are legal or illegal. Explain.

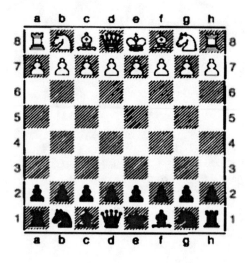

Look at the above chessboard. Is this board properly set up? Yes or no? Explain.

Clue: Look at where the queens are standing.

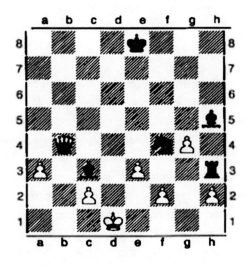

Look at the above board. How many of the black pieces can the white pawns capture? Explain why.

Clue: From this position, the pawn cannot capture the rook.

What to remember about the pawns:

1. A pawn has a value of one point.
2. Pawns cannot move backward.
3. Any pawn can move vertically one or two squares with an open move. They can then follow by moving one square with each proceeding move.
4. When a pawn advances to the eighth rank or first rank, it can become a queen or any other piece except another king or a pawn.
5. Pawns always capture diagonally.
6. White pawns always start on the second rank and the black pawn on the seventh rank.
7. Pawns cannot jump over another piece.
8. Pawns cannot capture two pieces with one move.
9. Pawns can execute pins on major pieces.
10. Pawns are the only pieces that capture pieces differently from how they move.

The following are some of the FIDE rules on pawns:

FIDE: Article 3.7

a. The pawn may move forward to the unoccupied square immediately in front of the same file, or

b. on its first move, the pawn may move as in (a); alternatively it may advance two squares along the same file provided both squares are unoccupied, or

c. the pawn may move to a square occupied by an opponent's piece, which is diagonally in front of it on the adjacent file, capturing that piece . . . .

e. When a pawn reaches the rank furthest from its starting position it must be exchanged as part of the same move for a new queen, rook, bishop or knight of the same color. The player's choice is not restricted to pieces that have been captured previously. This exchange of a pawn for another piece is called "promotion" and the effect of the new piece is immediate.

THE KNIGHT

A *knight* has a value of 3

Brief History of the Knight

The knight has changed very little through history. Since its inception, it has moved with a special jump. This movement has been in place before 700 AD. The Indians represented the knight as a mounted warrior with a shield and a sword. When the Arabs adopted and played this game, they simplified it. The knight became a cap with a triangular hole. Later in the Middle Ages, it was fashioned as a carved knight.

The knight on the chessboard also represents the professional soldier of the medieval times whose job was to protect persons of rank. During these earlier times, the cavalry never advanced head on, but their knights went around the back and attack from the side of their enemies.

Four knights are placed on the chessboard when it is completely set up. Two white knights and two dark-colored knights. The value of knights and the bishops are basically equal, but a fully developed knight or a bishop can cause real destruction especially when an opponent is under attack.

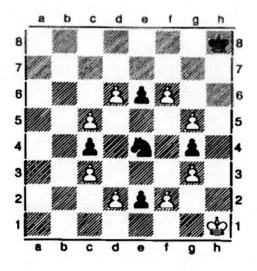

How to Move the Knight

Look at the knights and the white pawns that are placed on the board above. Notice that the knight can only capture the white pawns. The knights move in an L-shaped pattern—two squares in one direction then one square to either side in another direction. The knight is the only piece that can jump over other pieces on both sides of the board throughout the entire game. It must, however, move on a different color square when a move is made. A knight can capture any of its opponent pieces except for the king. The knights can move to any square on the board, but when placed on the outer edge or squares, they become weak. It is important that one moves the knights toward the center of the board, especially when making the first knight move.

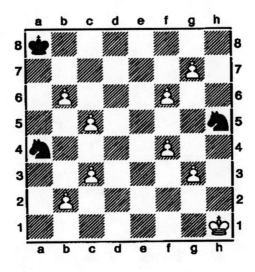

On this board, the knight is placed on the brim. This knight has less mobility than one that is placed in the center of the board. Notice, the knight on the left can only move to four possible squares. These squares are marked with white pawns. They are **b2, c3, c5,** and **b6.** The knight on the right can only move to **g3, f4, f6,** and **g7.**

Let us look at the different position and the mobility of a knight when it is moved toward the center of the board. Each pawn represents where a knight can move.

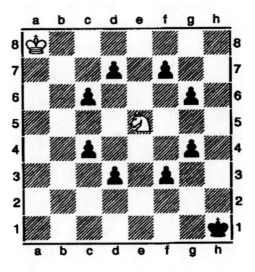

A knight that is placed near the center of the board has more mobility. Look at the knight above. This knight can move to eight different squares. The knight that was seen on the edge of the board was able to move only to four squares.

How to capture a piece with the knight

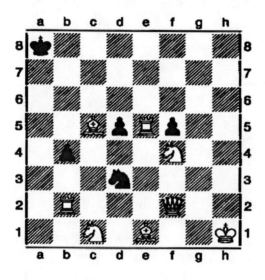

Look at the black knight on the board above. Notice that the black knight can capture any of the white pieces by moving in an *L-shaped* direction. This knight can move two squares vertically and one horizontally or one square horizontally and two squares vertically. Knights can also move one square vertically and two squares horizontally or two squares horizontally and one square vertically.

Set up your chessboard now; place some pieces on the board, and practice moving and capturing with the knight.

It is also important to note that the knight is the only piece on the board that can *jump over* other pieces to make a legal move such as capturing another piece. The knight can also move backward.

Fide: Article 3.6

The knight may move to one of the squares nearest to that on which it stands but not on the same rank, file or diagonal.

Summary Questions about the Knight

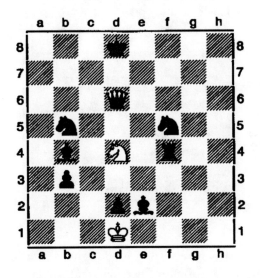

Look at the board above. The white knight is in a position to capture a number of pieces. Identify the pieces on the board that the knight can capture. Clue: All of the pieces cannot be captured by the knight.

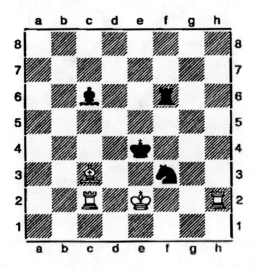

On the board above, it is black's turn to move. What is the best move for the knight?

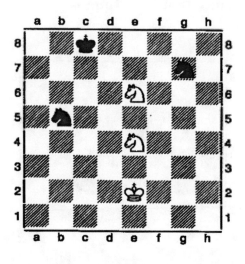

Look at the chessboard above. Four knights are sitting on this board. Two of the knights are strong and two are weak. What two knights are the strongest. Why? Explain.

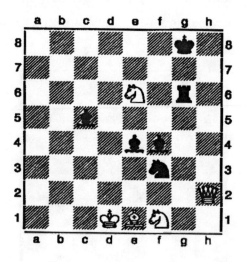

On the board above, tell how many pieces the white knights can capture. How many pieces can the black knight capture? What about on the next two boards? How many pieces can the knights capture?

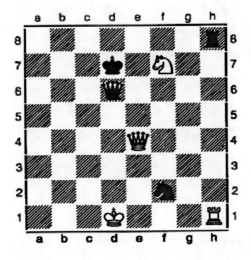

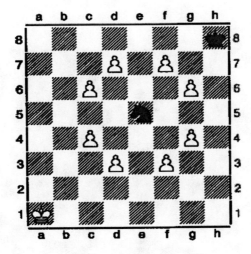

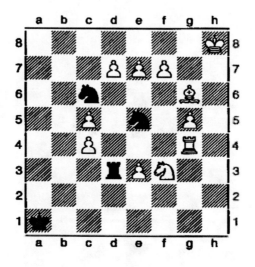

How many pieces can the knight that sits on **e5** capture? For this exercise, capture a piece then return the knight back to the original position on **e5**. Capture another piece until all of the pieces are removed from the board.

Chapter 4

THE BISHOP

      A bishop has a value of 3 points

Brief History of the Bishop

It is said that the bishop got its name during the medieval times because it represented the church. Bishops were important persons who worked their way up through the rank of the church and gained powerful positions. Others have claimed that the original bishops were actually sailing ships. Sailing ships never sailed straight. They tracked the wind left and right and sailed in diagonal positions.

The bishops are those pieces that have a point on top of their heads. Just like the knights, there are a total of four bishops that are placed on the chessboard at the beginning of a game. One bishop is placed on the **c1** square, the others on **f1**, **f8**, and **c8**. The bishops are the only pieces that move diagonally.

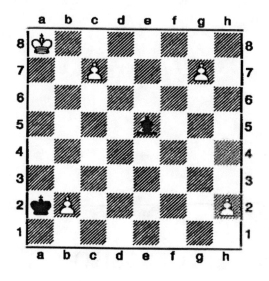

How to Move the Bishop

The bishop that is presented on the above chessboard can move and capture any piece on the diagonal lines. Those pieces that will be captured are pawns. If a bishop sits on the black squares, it can only move and capture pieces on the black squares. A bishop that sits on the white square can only move and capture pieces that are placed on the white squares. A bishop cannot cross over from one color to the next. A bishop that sits on the white square must remain on the white diagonal lines, and a bishop that sits on a dark square must remain on the black diagonal lines.

Unlike the knight, the bishop cannot jump over another piece. A bishop must wait for a pawn to move or be captured from the second rank or seventh rank to make its first move.

Both the knights and bishops are of equal value. They are not as valuable as rooks or queens. The bishop is faster in movement than the knight. A white bishop can occupy thirty-two squares, and a dark bishop can also move to occupy thirty-two squares.

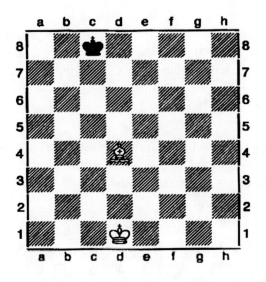

Look at the above chessboard. Notice how the bishop moves. It moves diagonally from **a1** to d4 and can go to h8. This move can be quite rapid.

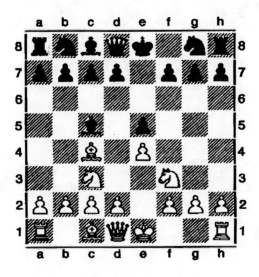

The white bishop that sits on **c4** moved from **f1**. This bishop must remain and move on all white squares along the diagonal path. It can capture any piece along this path and also move and capture backward. The black bishop can also move diagonally along the black diagonal path and capture any piece except an opponent's king. Note that the black bishop has moved from **f8** to **c5**.

Bishops that are developed can be very powerful pieces. Sometimes an opponent is forced to exchange a more powerful piece for a bishop or another piece in order to save the game.

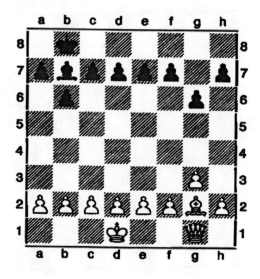

Note here on the board above, the white bishop that sits on the **g2** square can capture the black bishop that sits on the **b7** square. The black bishop that sits on the **b7** square can also capture the bishop that sits on the **g2** square.

FIDE: Article 3.2

The bishop may move to any square along a diagonal on which it stands.

Summary Questions about the Bishop

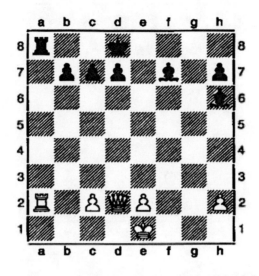

Look at the board above. What pieces can the black bishops capture? Are these pieces more valuable?

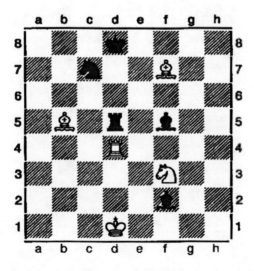

On the above board, what piece can the black bishop capture? What about the white bishop?

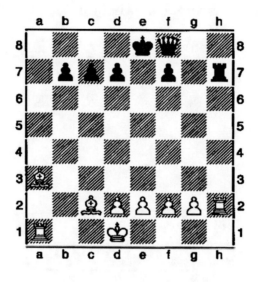

Above. What pieces can the white bishops capture?

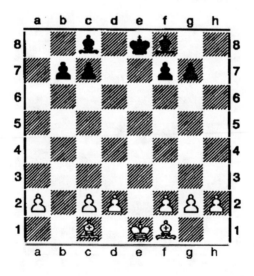

Look at the bishops on the previous board. Can the bishops capture any of the opponent's piece or pieces?

You now have realized that the bishops can capture pieces of different value, from the pawns to the queen. Bishops are considered to be minor pieces, but they can be very destructive when they are fully developed.

THE ROOK

    A rook has a value of 5 points

Brief History of the Rook

The rooks are some of the most valuable pieces that are charged with defending the king against aggressive attackers. One of the special moves that is used by the rook to defend the king is called castling. The rook is also capable of launching aggressive attacks, both horizontally and vertically, against opponent pieces. Rooks can capture pawns, knights, bishops, other rooks, and queens. Rooks cannot jump over any other piece. They must wait for the moving paths to be cleared to move or capture an opponent's piece. Like the knights, bishops, and queens, the rooks can move backward. They can also move on any of the sixty-four squares with rapid speed.

The rooks and queens are considered to be major pieces. This is so because any of these pieces can checkmate an opponent's king with the help of the king and without the help of another major or a minor piece.

The rook got its name from the Persians who once referred to their chariots as *rokh*. During the Persian war, the *rokh* or chariots were very effective in battle. These heavy-armored moving objects were fast, strong, well protected, and valuable. These chariots carried archers who were weapon bearers. They created havoc on the battlefields against their enemies.

When the Italians visited Persia, they adopted the word *rokh* and changed the name to *rocca*. Rocca in Italian, however, had a different meaning. It meant fortified tower. Later, those fortified towers began to shape like castles. Today, some people refer to rooks as castles. An experienced chess player, however, knows the distinct difference. Castle or castling usually refers to a position on the chessboard. It is a special move between the rook and the king. The rooks, on the other hand, are the pieces that are placed on **a1, h1, a8**, and **h8** at the beginning of the game.

All rooks can move vertically, horizontally, and backward along open files. They are most powerful in the end games when they are not obstructed by other pieces, especially the little pawns. Rooks cannot move or capture any piece on any diagonal square

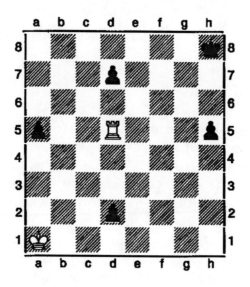

How to Move the Rook

The setting on the board above is designed to show how the rook moves. Notice that the rook is placed on the **d5** square and is surrounded by four pawns. The rook can move both horizontally and vertically and capture any of the black pawns. The rook can also move backward.

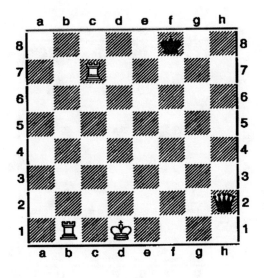

Look at the chessboard above. The rooks can move both vertically and horizontally. The white rook that sits on the **b1** square can make a very effective move by moving vertically to the **b8** square. When this move is executed, the *black king* has no escape route. The *king* is trapped. This is called *checkmate*.

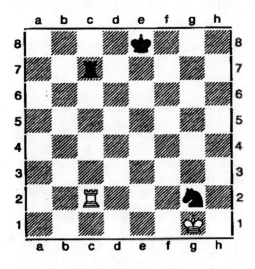

Look at the positions of the white rook above. This rook can capture either the black rook or the knight.

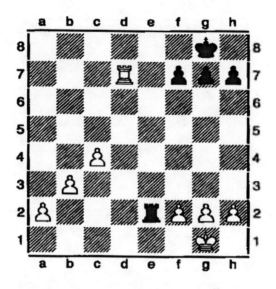

On the previous board is another example of the how the rook can move vertically and horizontally. The white rook first moved from **d7** to **d8,** trying to trap the king. The black rook will interpose by moving from **e2** to **e8**. White will then capture the black rook horizontally by moving from the **d8** square to the **e8** square. The *black king* is trapped. The game ends. This is example of *checkmate.* This mating process will be discussed in a later chapter.

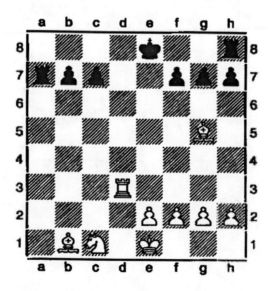

The white rook on the previous board is getting ready to make a direct attack on the black king by moving to **d8.** When the rook moves to **d8,** the player will say "Checkmate," meaning that the king is trapped. Note that the rook is protected by the bishop. The game is over.

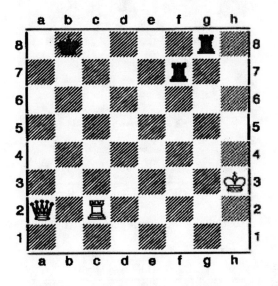

Look at the board above. It is black's turn to move. What is the best move for black? Notice that if the rook that sits on **f7** moves to **h7**, the *white king* would be trapped. That would be a *checkmate*.

It is important to note that the rooks are considered to be major pieces. They are the second most valued pieces on the board next to the queen.

FIDE: Article 3.3

The rook may move to any square along the file or the rank on which it stands.

Summary questions about the Rook

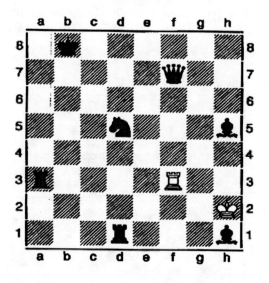

On the board above, how many pieces can the white rook capture?

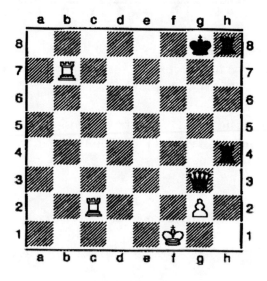

Look at the position on the previous board. What is the best move for the *white rook*? Explain

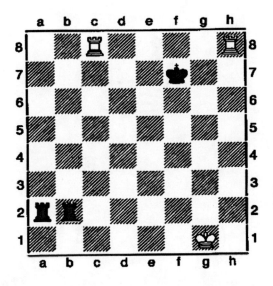

Look at the position on the above board. It is black's turn to move. What is the best move for any of the black rooks? Explain.

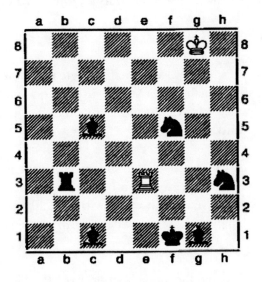

Look at the position on the above board. What piece or pieces can the white rook capture?

THE QUEEN

Each of the above queen has a value of 7 points

Brief History of the Queen

The queen is, by far, the most powerful single piece on the chessboard. When the game starts, each player starts with one queen, but as the game progresses, that player can obtain more queens when pawns advance on the eighth or first ranks.

Today, the queen represents a woman, but when the game first started, there was no piece that represented a queen or a female. The queen, as we know it today, was a man who was the closest advisor to the king. In Persia, that special male advisor was called *Firzan* who served for the safety of the king.

The Arabs who learned the game of chess from the Persians interpreted the figure standing next to the king as a queen and change the name of the piece to a queen. In the early days, the Firzan was not as powerful as our present queen. It was only allowed to move in one direction, and that was diagonally.

The Spaniards learned the game of chess from the Arabs. The Arabs once controlled southern Spain and as such, spread their cultural influence in this European country. As the Spaniards adopted the game, they develop, refined, and gave more power and importance to the queen.

During the fifteenth century, many women in Spain and other parts of Europe held leadership and influential position in their societies. This sphere of influence could be a main reason why the queen became so powerful.

Today, the queen is the most powerful piece to stand proudly on the board next to the king. She defends her king and fights off attackers. She is powerful, swift, wise, quite mobile, protective, and vicious.

One queen is equal in value to two rooks. A queen can move diagonally, vertically, backward, side to side, and to as many cleared squares on the board. It can capture pieces in any straight direction as long as the specific paths to those pieces are cleared.

The queen cannot jump over another piece. It must wait for a pawn to move before it can be activated. It is important to note that all pieces on the board, including the king, can capture a queen. When an opponent's queen is captured, without a queen exchange, the offensive and defensive blow is usually severe.

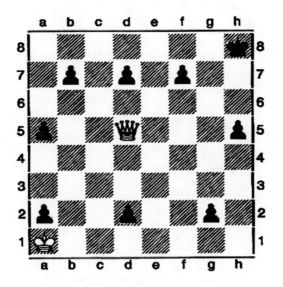

How to Move the Queen

The setting on the board above is designed to show how the queen moves. Notice that the queen is sitting in the center of the board. Notice also that there are many pawns that surround the queen. The queen can capture any of those pawns. The queen can move and capture vertical, horizontal, and diagonal lines. It can also move backward.

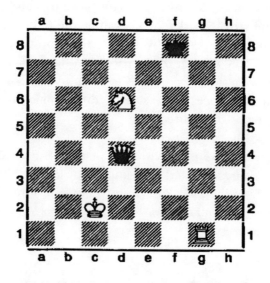

On the board above, the queen can capture the rook diagonally or the knight on the vertical line.

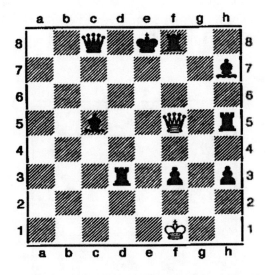

On the board above, notice the position of the white queen. This queen is in a position to capture as many as eight pieces. Notice that the *queen* can move diagonally, vertically, horizontally, and backward.

On the next chessboard, the queen has delivered a compelling blow on the *black king* by moving to **h7**. The *king* is totally trapped. It cannot move anyplace. This is called checkmate. Both the bishop and the queen have worked together to ensure a checkmate.

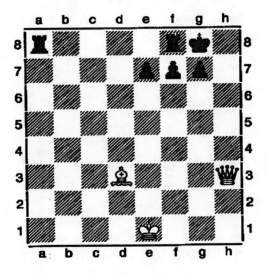

It is important to note that when the chessboard is set up correctly, the white queen must always be placed on the white square (**d1**) and the black queen sits on the black square (**d8**). On the board below, the two queens are standing on their original squares.

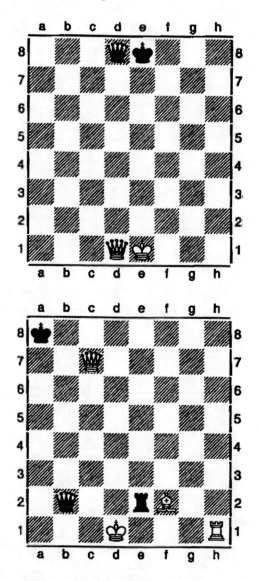

On the previous board, the white queen can make a very important move. Do you see this move? The best move for white is to force a checkmate by moving the queen to the **a7** square. The bishop is protecting the queen.

FIDE: Article 3.4

The queen may move to any square along the file, the rank or a diagonal on which it stands.

Summary Questions about the Queen

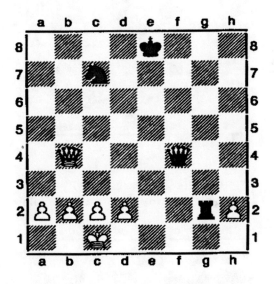

On the board above, the black queen is poised to make a very important move. What is the best move for black? Note, this move would lead to checkmate. Explain.

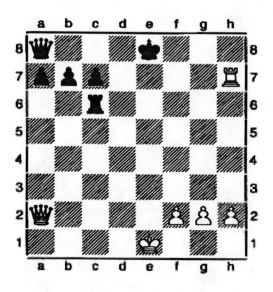

On the board above, the white queen has a very important move. Can you find this move? Clue: this move would lead to checkmate. Explain.

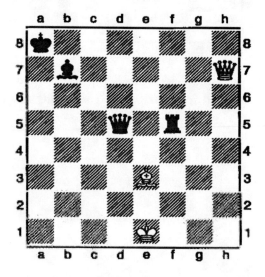

On the previous page, the white queen is in a position to make a very decisive move. Do you see the move for the white queen? Clue: this move will lead to a checkmate. Explain.

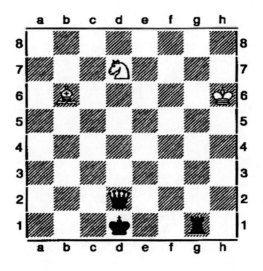

On the board above, the black queen is in a position to make a very decisive move. This move would lead to checkmate. Do you see the move? Explain.

Chapter 5

THE KING

**The king is a very important piece, but it has no point value.
The king cannot be traded. It does not leave the chessboard.**

Brief History of the King

The king is the main authority figure on the board that is protected by a number of major and minor pieces. The king is the highest piece on the chessboard. It stands above all of the other pieces with usually a cross on its head. It is the most important, but not the most powerful piece on the chessboard. The inventors of chess designed a figure for each arm of service. The *king* first represented the Indian emperor. This king was a wise ruler and not a warrior. The wars were fought by the generals, and the empire was defeated when the king was captured. This is why the game is won only when the enemy king is trapped. The king is never taken off the board. The main objective of each opponent is to corner the king so that it cannot escape.

In the game of chess, many pieces have sacrificed themselves to save the king from various attacking forces. The king has a lot of mobility, but its overall movement is very slow. It has the ability, however, to defend itself by capturing the opponent's pieces. It has the ability to move horizontally, vertically, diagonally, and backward one square at a time.

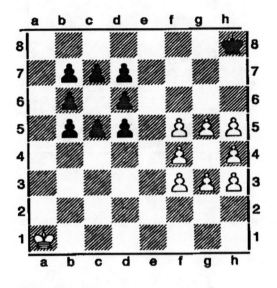

How to move the King

The board above is designed to show how a king moves. If the white king is placed on the **c6**—in the middle of the black pawns—this king would be able to capture any of the pawns that surrounds it. If the black king is placed on the **g4** square—in the middle of the white pawns—that king would be able to capture any of those black pawns. Notice the king can move horizontally, vertically, diagonally, and backward one square each move.

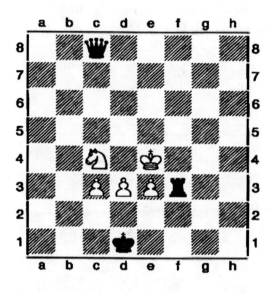

On the previous chessboard, the white king can move diagonally and capture the black rook.

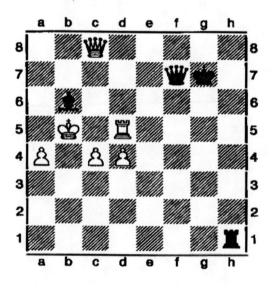

On the previous chessboard, the white king can move vertically and capture the unprotected bishop.

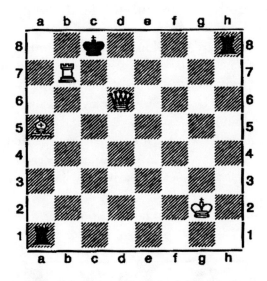

Look at the chessboard above. The black king is in a position to move diagonally and capture the rook. The rook is unprotected.

Special King Move—Castling

Castling is a special defensive move that is designed to protect one's king from an attack. This move was invented in the 1500s to help speed up the game and to help balance the offense and defense. These are the following rules that apply to castling:

1. This move can only occur if there are no standing pieces between the king and the rook.
2. The king cannot move from its original position.
3. The rook that makes the castling move cannot move from its original position.
4. The king cannot be in check or passes the line of check.
5. The king must be touched first then move two squares horizontally. The rook is then moved to the square that is opposite to the king.
6. If one castles on the king side, the king will move from the **e1** square to the **g1** square, and the rook that sits on the **h1** square will move to the **f1** square. If one is playing the dark colors pieces, the king will move from **e8** to **g8,** and the rook that sits on **h8** will move to **f8**.

7. When one castles on the queen side, the white king must move diagonally two spaces from **e1** to the **c1** square, and the rook that sits on the **a1** square would move to the **d1** square.

8. If one is playing the dark colors, the king would move from **e8** to **c8,** and the rook that stands on **a8** would move to **d8**.

9. Castling can only be done once in a game, and it is the only time the king can move twosquares.

10. Even though both the rook and the king move to a different position on the board, the castling moves are considered to be one move.

11. It is always advisable to castle early to avoid a quick open attack on your king.

12. Protect your king first then launch your attack.

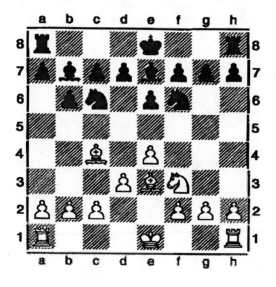

On the previous chessboard, the kings are poised to castle either on the king or the queen side. Notice the empty spaces between the rooks and the kings on both sides.

On the chessboard below, the kings have castled on the queen sides. These are the longer sides of the board.

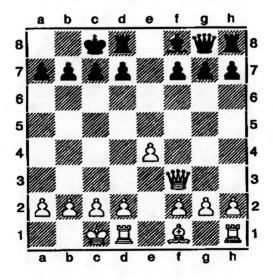

Note here that the kings have moved two squares horizontally to the left, and the rooks have moved three squares horizontally to the right. These moves are done at the same time.

When performing this move, it is important to touch the *king first;* move it to its intended location, then touch the *rook* and also move it to its intended location. One can also castle legally by holding the king and the rook at the same time and then move both pieces to their respective new positions.

It is important to note here that if a rook is touched before the king, and then it is moved to execute a castle, that move is considered to be a rook move. Moving the king after the rook is touched is an *illegal castle* move.

On the chessboard below, the king has castled on the king side. The king has moved two squares horizontally to the right, and then the rook moved two squares horizontally to the left.

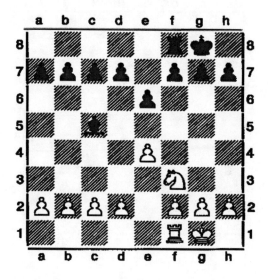

Notice here that the white king is protected by the rook, knight, and a number of pawns. Both players have castled early and will now begin to launch an offense.

FIDE: Article 3.8 (*Official rule on castling*)

There are two different ways of moving the king, by:

1. **moving to any adjoining square not attacked by one or more of the opponent's pieces.**
2. **"Castling" This is a move of the king and either rook of the same color on the same rank, counting as a single move of the king and executed as follows: the king is transferred from its original square two squares towards the rook, then that rook is transferred to the square the king has just crossed."**

Losing the right to castle:

FIDE: Article 3.8

The right for castling has been lost

> (1) if the king has already moved, or
> (2) with a rook that has already moved.

Castling is prevented temporarily

> (1) if the square on which the king stands, or the square which it must cross, or the square which it is to occupy, is attacked by one or more of the opponent's pieces.
> (2) if there is any piece between the king and the rook with which castling is to be effected.

Article 4.4

> a. If a player deliberately touches his king and rook he must castle on that side if it is legal to do so.
> b. If a player deliberately touches a rook and then his king he is not allowed to castle on that side on that move. He must move the first piece that was touched.

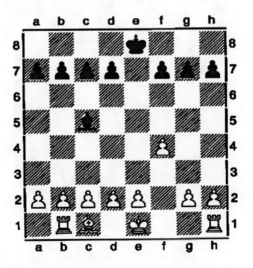

Notice on the board above, white is aiming to castle but cannot because it will be crossing over the bishop diagonal line.

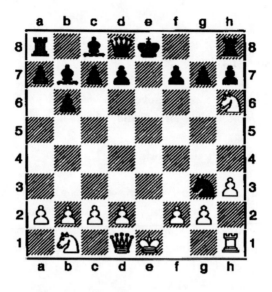

On the chessboard above, both kings would like to castle on the king side but can't because they will be making an illegal move by crossing over the **f1** and **g8** squares. These two squares are the check squares for the knight.

Summary Questions about the King

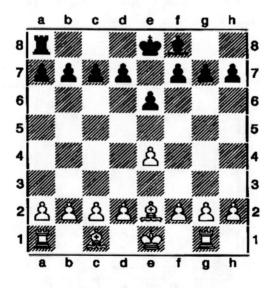

Look at the board above. One of the sides is prepared for castle on the next move. Can you identify which color? Explain.

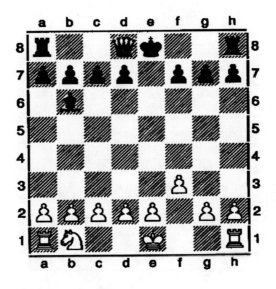

On the chessboard above, one of the sides is prepared to castle. Can you identify that side? Explain why the other color cannot castle.

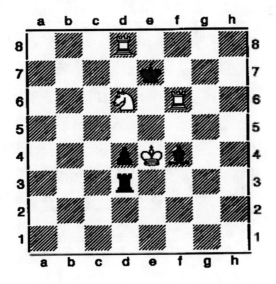

On the board above, how many pieces can the black and white kings capture?

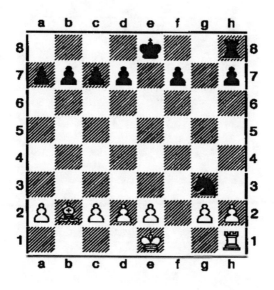

On the previous board can the two kings castle?

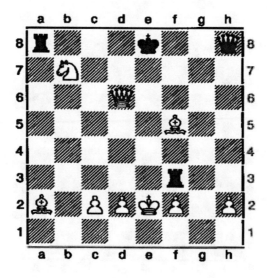

Look at the chesssboard above. One of the kings is in a position to capture an important piece. Do you see the king and the move?

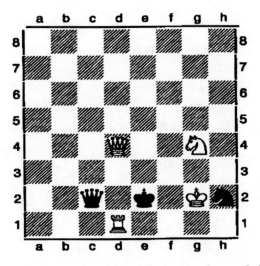

Take a close look at the chessboard above. One of the kings is in a position to capture a piece. Do you see the king and the move?

It is again important to remember that the king can become an attacking piece. The king is not a helpless piece. The king can also move in all directions one square at a time.

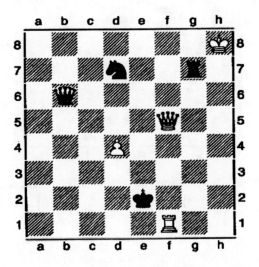

On the previous board, one of the kings is in a position to capture an important piece. Can you identify the king and the piece that it can capture? Explain why this capture can be made.

Understanding the value of the pieces

Fill out the following information below:

Computing the values of the pieces

1 pawn + 1 knight + 1 bishop =   _____ points

2 knights + 1 rook + 1 bishop =   _____ points

2 rooks + 2 pawns + queen =   _____ points

2 queens + 1pawn +1 knight =   _____ points

1 queen + 1 pawn+ 1 bishop =   _____ points

Exchanging of pieces/Best Choices:

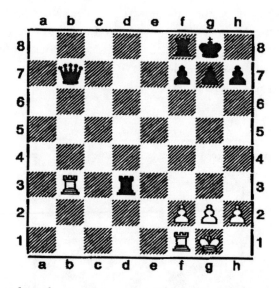

Look at the board on the previous page. The white rook is poised to capture either the black queen or the black rook. Which of the two pieces would you capture?

Answer: The best choice would be to take the queen. The queen is far more valuable than the rook.

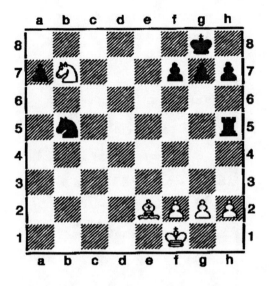

On the board above, which piece should the bishop capture? Which of the two pieces would you capture?

Answer: Capture the rook. This is more valuable.

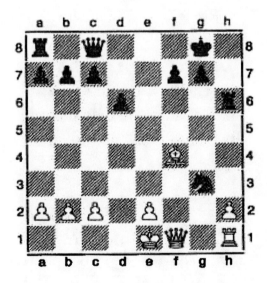

Look at the chessboard above. The white bishop is in a position to take either the knight or the rook. Which of the two pieces would you capture?

Answer: The best piece to capture in this exchange would be the knight. Notice that even though the knight is valued less than the rook, the knight is in a position to cause more damage to the white than the black rook.

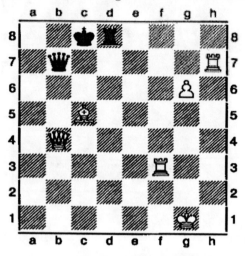

Look at the board above. The black queen is poised to capture either one of the rooks or the opposing queen. Which piece would you capture?

Answer: The best piece to capture in this position would be the rook that is standing on the **f3** square.

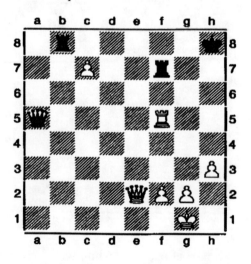

Look carefully at the board above. The black queen is in a position to capture the rook on the **f5** square and the pawn that is standing on the **c7** square. Which of the two pieces would capture?

Answer: Note that if the black queen captures the rook, the pawn will capture the rook on **b8** and would promote to a queen or a rook. This positional advantage would lead to a checkmate with the help of the other pieces. With this position, the best piece to capture is the pawn that is placed on the seventh rank.

Summary Questions on Correct Exchanges

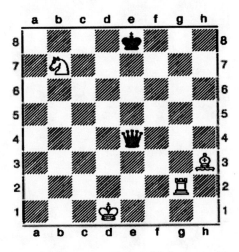

On the board above, which piece should the queen capture, the rook or the knight?

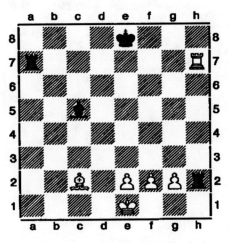

On the previous chessboard, the white rook has a choice between capturing the black rook on **h2** or the rook on **a7**. Which one would you capture and why?

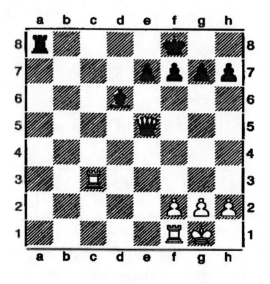

On this board should the queen capture the rook on **c3** or the pawn on **h2**?

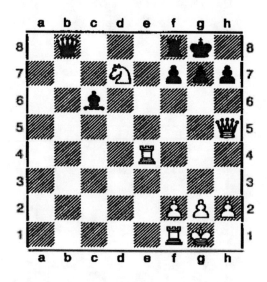

On the board above, the black bishop has a choice of capturing the white rook that sits on **e4** or the knight that sits on **d7**. Which piece should be captured?

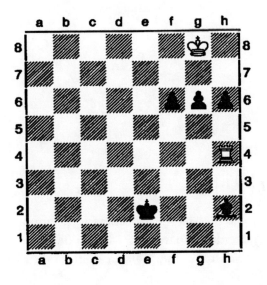

On this board the white rook has a choice of capturing the pawn that sits on **h6** or the bishop that sits on **h2**. Which is the best move?

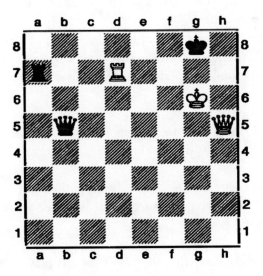

On the board above, the rook has a choice between capturing black rook or move to the **d8** square. Which move is the best move?

Chapter 6

Who should play first?

If players are participating in a chess tournament, the tournament arbitrator usually decides who will play what color. If two players are getting ready to engage in a casual game, a simple democratic process can be used. Here are some ideas:

1. Before the game begins, both players can decide who will play what color.
2. One of the two players can flip a coin, and the winner of the toss can choose a color.
3. One of the two players can place a black and a white pawn behind the back, and then the other player can touch one of the hands. The hand that is touched by the player would determine what color that player should play.
4. The chessboard can be placed on a table upside down; when the board is flipped over, the player who is sitting at the **a1** rank side would play white and the other player plays black.

It is important that both players develop their own simple method. The method that is selected must give each player a fifty-fifty chance of selecting one of the colors.

The rules of chess state that the player who is playing the white pieces *must play first*. This is important because white has the first offensive move. This offensive move is important because that person can dictate how the game should be played.

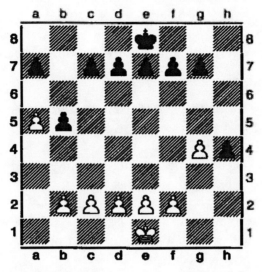

Now that we have looked at how to move each of the chess pieces, let us conduct a general review of the past information.

Review

The following questions are designed to provide more clarity, foster discussion, and determine certain levels of competency. You are expected to answer at least 80 percent of the questions correctly.

At the end of each question, circle one of the following: a. always, b. sometimes, or c. never. Try to answer these questions without looking at the answers. The answers to these questions are located on the page that comes after the questions. (Each question values four points)

Questions

1. At the beginning of the game of chess, any color can move first.
   a. Always   b. Sometimes   c. Never

2. The king has more point value than any other piece on the chessboard.
   a. Always   b. Sometimes   c. Never

3. Pawns eat diagonally and sometimes vertically.
   a. Always   b. Sometimes   c. Never

4. Pawns move vertically and capture diagonally.
   a. Always   b. Sometimes   c. Never

5. Some pawns can move backward in a chess game.
   a. Always   b. Sometimes   c. Never

6. At the opening of a game, a pawn is the only piece that can move first.
   a. Always   b. Sometimes   c. Never

7. When a pawn advances to the last rank (white eighth rank, black first rank) a player can ask for any major piece.
   a. Always   b. Sometimes   c. Never

8. Bishops move diagonally and eat vertically.
   a. Always   b. Sometimes   c. Never

9. A bishop that sits on a black square can sometimes capture an opponent on a white square.
   a. Always   b. Sometimes   c. Never

10. Bishops are the tallest pieces that sit on a chessboard.
    a. Always   b. Sometimes   c. Never

11. A bishop cannot capture a queen because it is not as important as the queen.
    a. Always   b. Sometimes   c. Never

12. At the beginning of a chess game, rooks and bishops are equal in value.
    a. Always   b. Sometimes   c. Never

13. The bishop and the rook can move and capture backward.
    a. Always   b. Sometimes   c. Never

14. When the chessboard is set up, the square **h1** should always appear on the left lower corner for the person who is playing white.
    a. Always   b. Sometimes   c. Never

15. Queens can move in all directions including a L-shaped direction like the knight.
    a. Always   b. Sometimes   c. Never

16. In the game of chess, a queen cannot capture another queen.
    a. Always   b. Sometimes   c. Never

17. The white king can capture a black queen.
    a. Always   b. Sometimes   c. Never

18. A chess game ends when one king captures the other king.
    a. Always   b. Sometimes   c. Never

19. Rooks move and capture horizontally and vertically.
    a. Always   b. Sometimes   c. Never

20. One can execute a castle while the king is in check.
    a. Always   b. Sometimes   c. Never

21. En passant is permitted on any square on the chessboard.
    a. Always   b. Sometimes   c. Never

22. When one castles, the rook is permitted to move first.
    a. Always   b. Sometimes   c. Never

23. When the chessboard is set up, the white queen should sit on a white square, and the black queen on black square.
    a. Always   b. Sometimes   c. Never

24. A king can castle on either side of the Chessboard: on the king side or the queen side.
    a. Always   b. Sometimes   c. Never

25. The queen is the tallest piece on the chessboard.
    a. Always   b. Sometimes   c. Never

Answers to the previous questions

1. *Never*   The player who is playing white must move first.
2. *Never*   The king is a very important piece, but it has no traded value like the queen, rook, bishop, knight or pawns.
3. *Never*   The pawns do eat diagonally but never vertically.
4. *Always*   The pawns always move vertically and capture diagonally
5. *Never*   Pawns never capture or move backward.
6. *Sometimes* The pawns do move first sometimes, but the knight can also move first.
7. *Always*   A player can ask for any major piece when a pawn reaches the eighth or the first rank.
8. *Never*   Bishops always capture on the diagonal lines.
9. *Never*   A bishop cannot cross over to another diagonal color line.
10. *Never*   The king is always the tallest piece.
11. *Always*   A bishop can always capture a queen.
12. *Never*   The rook has a higher value than the bishop.
13. *Always*   Both the bishop and the rooks can move and capture backward.
14. *Never*   If you are a right-handed person, that square should always appear at the lower right corner.
15. *Never*   Queens never move in an L direction.
16. *Always*   A queen can capture any other opposing-colored queen when the opportunity arises.
17. *Always*   A white king can always capture a white queen as long as the king's move is a legal move.
18. *Never*   A king cannot legally capture another king.
19. *Always*   Rooks can legally move and capture vertically and horizontally.
20. *Never*   Castling through or while the king is in check is an illegal move.
21. *Never*   En passant is executed on the sixth and on the third ranks.

22. *Never*   When the rook moves first, it is legally a rook move.
23. *Always*   The queens must sit on their own color squares.
24. *Always*   The king can castle on any side of the chessboard when the opportunity arises.
25. *Never*   The king is always the tallest piece on the chessboard.

Chapter 7

Chess Symbols

Certain marks are used in chess to represent certain ongoing ending activities. If you are a driver of a vehicle, you must become familiar with certain road signs to avoid accidents. If you are an architect, you are expected to use certain symbols when drawing a house plan. These symbols will help people interpret meanings without reading many pages of detailed work.

The following are some of the many symbols that are used in chess when a game is recorded:

When placed at the end of a move:

+	It means check
+ +	Double check
O-O	Castle on the king side
O-O-O	Castle on the queen side
#	Checkmate
1-0	White wins
O-1	Black wins
½-½	Game is a draw
?	Weak move
dis	Discovered check
!	Good move
!!	Very good move
?!	Risky move

Algebraic Notation

Black

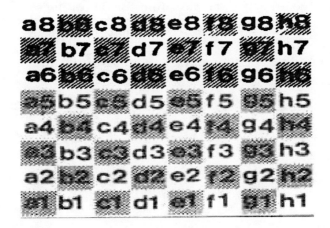

White

Individuals who are learning the game of chess should also learn how to record their moves. The following are some of the reasons why it is important to record one's game:

1. A recorded game allows the player to analyze the entire game after it has been played.
2. If a dispute occurs while the game is in progress, the arbitrator or the two parties can reconstruct the game from the beginning by using the recorded information.
3. The recorded game can be used as proof that the game was played.
4. In many official tournament games, all players are required to record each game. This information can be used as part of the historical record.
5. Copies to the game can be sent to other individuals who were not present while the game was played.

There are several forms of notations, but the one that is most popular and is used by most people today is the algebraic method of recording.

First, the recorded paper is clearly marked accordingly:

Event _____

Section _____ Round _____ Board _____ Date _____

White _____ Black _____

White	Black
1. _____	1. _____
2. _____	2. _____
3. _____	3. _____
4. _____	4. _____
5. _____	5. _____
6. _____	6. _____
7. _____	7. _____
8. _____	8. _____

One side is white and the other is black. The white section is located on the left-hand side of the paper and the black is on the right. The paper that is used is usually numbered from 1, signifying the first move, to 60 and beyond, to signify the number of possible moves that could be recorded in a complete game.

After the paper is properly filled-out and the clock is hit by the person who is playing the black pieces, the person who is playing the white pieces will make a move, hit the clock, and then record the move.

When one is recording a game, the beginning letter of the piece that is being moved must be written first, then the square on which the piece will be placed second, followed by a specific number that identifies the square. When writing a pawn move, the letter p does not have to be written first:

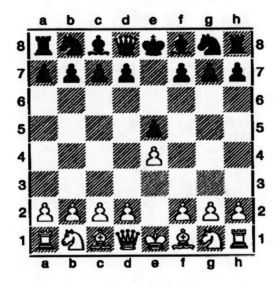

On the board above, the white pawn has moved first. Black also has moved a pawn on the first move. The moves should be written as:

White	Black
1. e4	**1. e5**

Notice in this example the white pawn that starts on the second rank (**e2**) advanced vertically two squares to the fourth rank (**e4**). The pawn moves *could simply* be written as **e4**. It is understood that only one piece on the board can advance to the **e4** square.

On the other side of the board, the opponent responded by moving black two squares to **e5**. The black pawn that started on the seventh rank at (**e7**) advanced vertically two squares to **e5**.

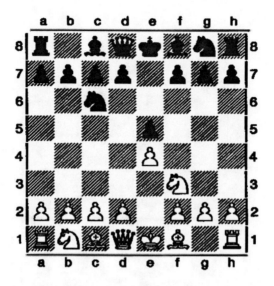

On the board above, white has made the second move. The knight has moved from **g1** to **f3.** Black responded by moving the black knight from **b8** to **c6.**

This second move should be written as **Nf3** and **Nc6**. Notice that a letter *n* signifies that the knights have moved to the **f3** and **c6** squares.

White	Black
1. **e4**	1. **e5**
2. **Nf3**	2. **Nc6**

Again, when another piece, such as the bishop, queen, rook, or king is moved, the first letter that identifies those pieces should be written *first,* then the number of the square where that piece landed should follow. Example, if the bishop moves from the **f1** square to **c5** that move should be written as **Bc5**. If a rook moves from **h8** to **h2**, that move should be written as **Rh2**. If a king moves from **e1** to **e2**, that move should be written as **Ke2**. If the king castles on the king side that move should be written as **0-0** and on the queen side **0-0-0**.

Writing Castle moves:

0-0   when one castles on the king side.

0-0-0 when one castles on the queen side

When capturing any piece, the symbol of an x should be recorded. For example, if a queen moves from the **e1** rank and captures a bishop on the **e7** rank, that move should be written as **Qxe7**.

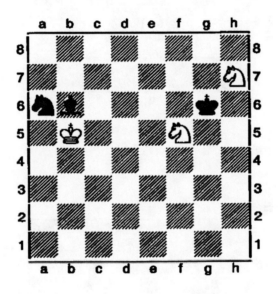

On the chessboard above, it is black's turn to move. The black king can capture either knights. In this case, one must distinguish which knight was taken by the king. If the king captures the knight on the **h** file, then it is written **Kxh7** and on the **f** file, it should be written as **Kxf5**.

On the other side of the board, if the white king captures the black bishop, it should written as **Kxb6,** and if the black knight is captured, that move should be written as **Kxa6**.

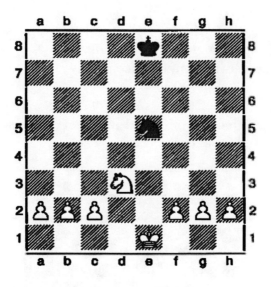

On the board above, if the black knight captures knight, it should be written as **NxN**

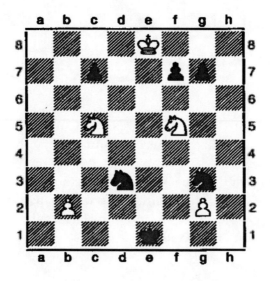

Look at the position on the above board. If one of the white knights captures one of the black knights, that move cannot be written as **NxN**. More specific information must be presented. With just **NxN**, no one really knows which of the two knights captured the black knight. With this move, one must specify which of the two knights. If for example, the knight that sits on the **f5** square captures the knight that sits on the **g3** square that notation should be written as **Nf5xN**. Only one knight can be moved from the **f** file position and make a capture.

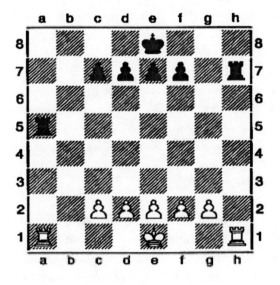

On the board above, it is white's turn to move. Either white rook can capture any of the exposed black rooks. The move cannot be written as **RxR** but rather **Ra1xR** or **Rh1w**.

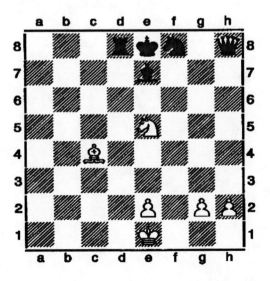

What is a Check?

Check is not a form of checkmate. Check is a signal to the opponent that the king is in under a direct attack, and it must be moved out of that position either by moving the king, moving a piece to block the attack, or by capturing the attacking piece. Any of the major or minor pieces can check a king.

FIDE: Article 3.9

The king is said to be "in check" if it is attacked by one or more of the opponent's pieces, even if such pieces are constrained from moving to that square because they would then leave or place their own king in check. No piece can be moved that will ever expose the king of the same color to check or leave that king in check."

What is Checkmate?

Checkmate is the term used when the king is trapped. The king is trapped when it is in check and cannot "get out of check" even when all defensive actions are taken. The word check is used when the king is under direct attack from a piece, and *checkmate* means that the game is over.

As mentioned earlier, the major objective of any chess game is to trap the king. This is the ultimate prize. When the king is cornered, the game is over. The term that is used to give the signal that the game is over is "checkmate."

Any of the chess piece can checkmate a king with the help of other pieces. A chess game could also end if a player leans the king on the board and say "I resign." This action is taken when that player sees the end in sight and extends the courtesy to the other player by not prolonging the game.

This type of etiquette is not applied in all games. Some players will purposely prolong a game with the hope that the attacker would make a major mistake or be forced into a stalemate or a draw.

On many occasions, I have seen a number of games where players gained a slight initiative and are in positions to force checkmates in one or two moves, but prolonged checkmate with a weak move, and then suffer a loss. Opponents could take advantage of each mistake and turn a losing position into a win.

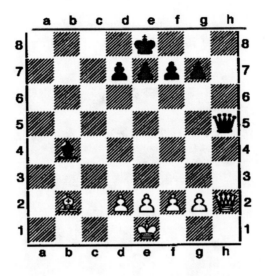

Look at the previous board carefully. It is white's turn to move. Naturally, the first instinct is to capture the white queen. The single important question that should be asked is "Could a different move be executed that would be more effective?" The best move for the white queen is not to capture the black queen but to move to **b8**. When the queen moves to **b8**, that would be a checkmate. This move should be written as **Qa8#**

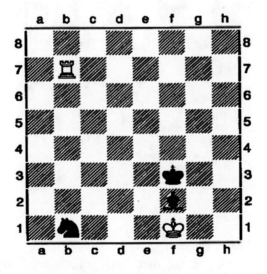

Look at the above board carefully. It is black's turn to move. The objective here is to make sure that the *king* does not escape. What happens if the *knight* moves to **d2** *with a check*? The king cannot move. That is a checkmate! This move should be written as **Nd2#.**

Look at the next chessboard. How can white checkmate black in two moves?
Answer: **Rg8**—the queen will block; rook then captures the queen. Mate!

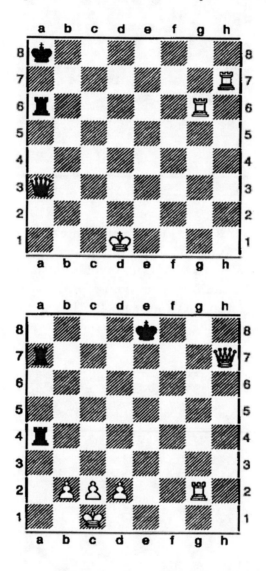

On the board above, it is black's turn to move. Notice that the two rooks
are lined up and are working together. It is black's turn to move. Should black
capture the white queen, or should the rook on **a4** move to **a1**? Think about
this. The objective here is not to capture pieces but to go for the checkmate.
The rook on **a4** moving to **a1** would be the decisive move. That is *checkmate*.

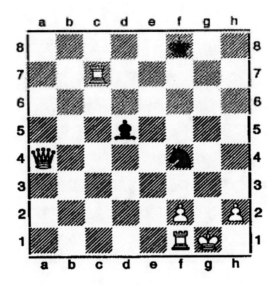

On the board above, it is black's turn to move. What is the best move for black? Do you see the checkmate in one move? Notice that the king is trapped if the knight moves either to **h3** or **e2**. Either move is checkmate.

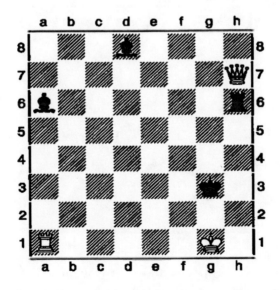

What is the best move for black on the above board? Answer: **B** to **b6**. That is checkmate

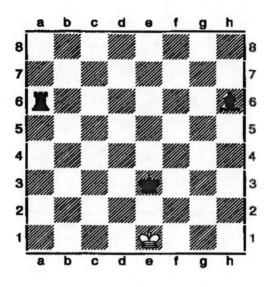

Look at the board above. It is black's turn to move. What will be the best immediate move for black? Black wins with one move, and checkmate!

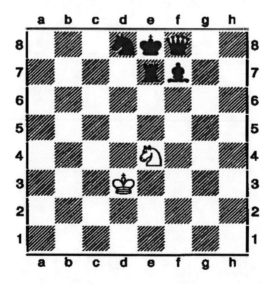

Look carefully at the board above. It is white's turn to move. Black clearly has more pieces on the board, but the pieces are poorly placed, and they are inactive. What is the best move for white? White wins! One move, and checkmate!

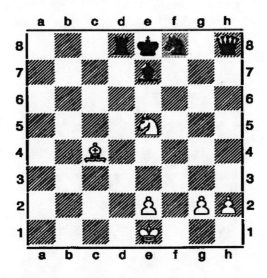

Look at the board above. It is white's turn to move. Notice that black has more valuable pieces on the board than white, but white has checkmate in one move. Do you see the checkmate?

What is a Stalemate?

A stalemate is a draw. This term is used when the king is not in check, and it cannot move without going into check, and no other piece on the board can move. Let us look at some examples of stalemate.

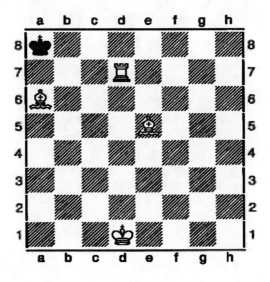

On the previous board, it is black's turn to move. The king cannot move into check, and no other black piece on the board can move. This is a stalemate.

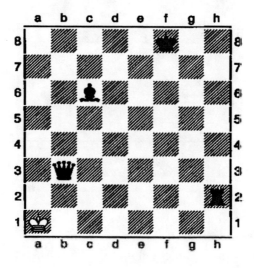

On the board above, the white king must move but cannot move into check. This is a stalemate.

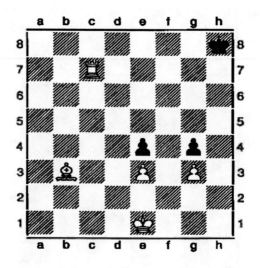

On the board above, black is in a stalemated position.

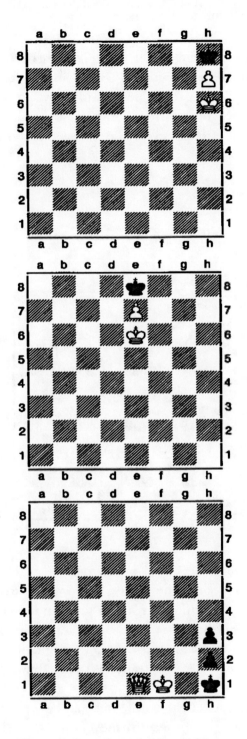

Look at the position on three boards above. These are some common end game positions. It is black's turn to move. In all three games, the black king cannot move. These are all stalemated position.

When a game is stalemated, both players receive half point each. Games can also end without a one-point victory for either side. These games are called draws. Some draws are achieved with three consecutive repetitive moves, the fifty-move rule or, when both players have insufficient material on the board to force a mate. With a draw, each player receives one-half of a point.

Forms of Draws

Three Repetitive Moves

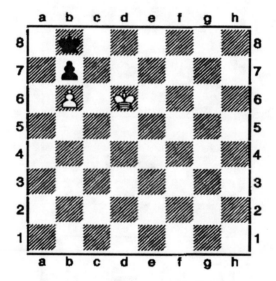

On the board above, it is black's turn to move. Black chooses to move the king to the **a8** square. The white king moves to **d7**. The black king moves again to **b8**. The white king moves to **d8** and then repeats the next move to **d7**. If black decide, for the third time, to move to **a8**, and the white king moves to **d8**, these same moves could continue forever. Once three repetitive moves are made, the position is then a draw.

The chess rules also state that the game may be *drawn* if each player has made at least the last fifty consecutive moves without the movement of any pawn and without any capture (**Article 5.2e**).

On many occasions, the person who is under attack and knows that there is very little hope of winning may refuse to resign. That person is hoping that the opponent makes a mistake and forces the king into a stalemated position. This is especially common when the defender has far less valued pieces on the board. In such a situation, both players can continue the game until one is checkmated or, in rare cases, both can agree to a draw. One of the FIDE rules states that "the game is drawn upon agreement between the two players during the game. This immediately ends the game."

Chapter 8

Opening Moves

The first move of any game is referred to as the opening move. This initial move is a very critical move. This single move can provide protection for the king, control the middle game, helps with the movement of different pieces, and can lead to a winning game.

Opening moves have been studied for hundreds of years. Books have been written about a single pawn move or a single opening.

Let us look briefly at some of these openings that are still used today by the casual, professional, and seriously minded players. It is important that chess players be aware of these openings and develop the proper strategies to defend against these offensive moves. It is advisable to practice any openings:

1. **Ruy Lopez**

This is called the Spanish opening. This game was named after Ruy Lopez, a sixteenth-century Spanish clergyman who was an avid chess player. The roots of this particular opening was found in writings dating back the 1490s. It is a favorite move of Bobby Fischer and Garry Kasparov, two of the modern world champions.

Here are a few of the opening moves to one of the many variations of the Ruy Lopez:

White	Black
1. e4	e5
2. Nf3	Nc6
3. Bb5	d6
4. O-O	Nf6
5. d4	Nxe4

Conduct further research on the many variations of this opening.

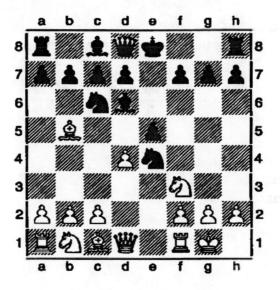

Giuoco Piano

This is an excellent way to open a chess game. The Giuoco Piano aims in a rapid development and a control for the center of the board while applying pressure on the **f7** pawn.

This game was named after an Italian chess player called Gioachino Greco who lived in the seventeenth century.

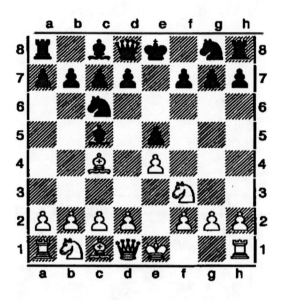

The following are some of the series of moves:

White	Black
1. **e4**	e5
2. **Nf3**	Nc6
3. **Bc4**	Bc5
4. **d3**	d6
5. **O-O**	Bg4
6. **Nc3**	Nd4
7. **Be3**	

Conduct further research on the many variations of the Giuoco Piano opening.

Sicilian Defence

One of the most popular opening that is played today is the Sicilian Defence. The research shows that 17 percent of all games between grandmasters and 20 percent of games in chess information database begins with this opening.

The earliest recorded notes on the Sicilian Defence date back to the sixteenth century by the Italian chess players Giulio Polerio and Gioachino Greco. The main variation of this game starts with white moving to **e4** and black responding with **c5**.Here are some further moves in one of the many variations of this opening:

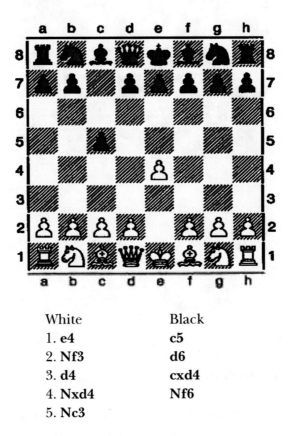

White	Black
1. **e4**	**c5**
2. **Nf3**	**d6**
3. **d4**	**cxd4**
4. **Nxd4**	**Nf6**
5. **Nc3**	

Conduct further research on the various variation of this opening.

The English Opening

The English opening derives its name from the English world champion, Howard Staunton who played it during his 1843 match. The main first opening line to this game is that white moves to **c4**.

It is the hope of white to control the center by gaining support from the side.

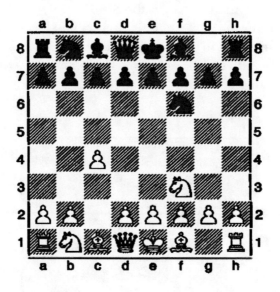

The following is one of the variations of this opening.

White	Black
1. c4	Nf6
2. Nc3	g6
3. d4	d5

Continue to study the English opening.

The Caro-Kann Defence

The Caro-Kann Defence is a common chess opening that starts with white moving to **e4** and then black responding to **c6**.

This opening is named after the English player Horation Caro and the Austrian Marcus Kann who analyzed this opening in 1886.

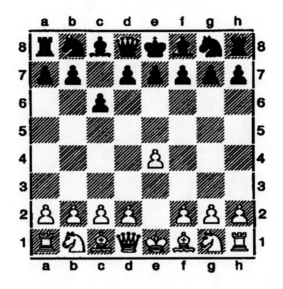

Here is one of the main variations to this opening:

White	Black
1. **e4**	**c6**
2. **d4**	**d5**
3. **Nc3**	**dxc4**
4. **Nxe4**	**Bf5**
5. **Ng3**	**Bg6**
6. **h4**	**h6**
7. **Nf3**	**Nd7**

Continue to study this opening

The French Defence

This opening starts with **e4** for white and **e6** for black. In this opening, black allows white to gain early control of the center and minimized the effectiveness of the bishop. Black on the other hand tries to build a wall of pawns. The development of this game can be traced back to Paris and London in 1834.

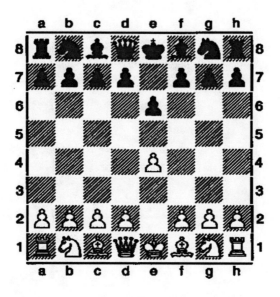

Earlier examples of the French opening do exist before 1834. However, here is one of the basic variations of this opening:

White	Black
1. e4	e6
2. d4	d5
3. Nc3	Nf6
4. Bg5	Be7
5. e5	Nfd7
6. Bxe7	Qxe7
7. f4	O-O

continue to study this opening.

King's Gambit

The King's Gambit is one of the oldest documented openings as it was examined by the seventeenth-century Italian chess player Giulio Polerio. In this opening, a pawn is sacrificed to divert the black e-pawn so as to build a stronger center.

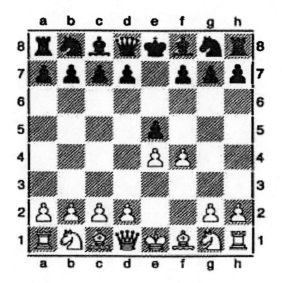

White	Black
1. e4	e5
2. f4	exf4
3. Nf3	d5

Important Opening Tips:

1. Avoid moving the same piece twice.
2. Develop your pieces early.
3. Develop your pieces before you attack.
4. Castle early.
5. Avoid doubling your pawns.
6. Move your knights toward the center of the board.
7. Avoid blocking the open squares for your pieces.
8. Analyze each move carefully. Think of action and consequences before a move is made and a piece is captured.

Chapter 9

Middle-Game Advantages

Gaining a slight advantage in any stage of the game is an advantage in itself. Some advantages are gained early in the opening moves, others in the middle game, and many in the end games. Let us examine some scenarios in the middle game and decide which side has the advantage.

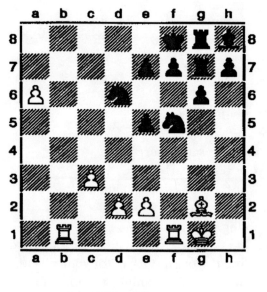

White Move

Look at this middle-game scenario on the previous board. Even though black has the more valuable pieces, the white is in a better position. White has the advantage in this game. The white pawn will advance to **a8** and then be awarded a queen.

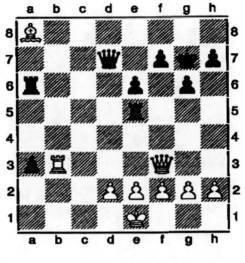

Black to Move

Look at this middle game above. Black has the clear advantage. Look at the advancing pawn on **a3**. Black will obtain a queen, or white will lose another piece.

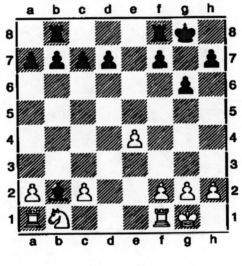

Black to Move

In this game, black has the advantage. Look at the black bishop. The white rook will be captured.

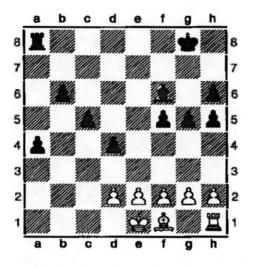

On the above board, black has the advantage. White is down three pawns, and black is advancing the pawn on the **a** file for another queen. Black should win this game if this advantage is maintained.

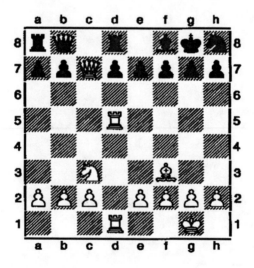

On the board above, both black and white have the same valued pieces. White, however, has a positional advantage. It is white's turn to move. Obviously, white will exchange the queen then win a few pawn by continuing with rook take pawn, exchanging the rooks, and applying additional pressure on the **b7** pawn. White should win this game if the advantage is maintained.

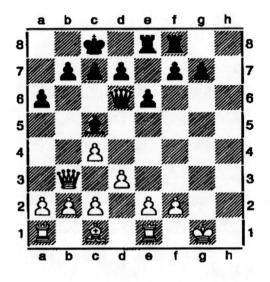

On the board above, both black and white have equal valued pieces, but black has the position advantage. The two black rooks are freed. They will begin to launch an attack shortly on the white king. The black queen and bishop are also standing by to assist.

Chess Tactics

A winning strategy is critical in every sport. Without such a plan, the gaining of an advantage or a win would be very difficult.

In chess, one of these strategies is called a tactic. Tactic in chess refers to a short sequence of well-calculated offensive moves. These moves are designed to limit the opponent's option of movement, which in the end results in meaningful gains.

There are different types of tactics such as a fork, pin, discovered check, double check, skewer, decoy, removing the guard, overload, deflection, and forcing a draw more. Let us look at some of these examples.

Different Types of Fork

The term *fork* is used in chess when a single piece is attacking two pieces. A fork can be executed by all chess pieces including the king. It is often said that when one is forked by a knight on a queen, or be forked by pawns, the effect can be devastating. Let us look at a few examples:

Pawn Fork,

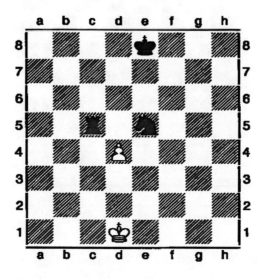

In the diagram above, look at the *white pawn*. The pawn is attacking both the knight and the rook at the same time. One of these more valued pieces will be captured by a little pawn. This is an example of a *pawn fork*.

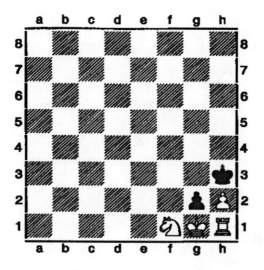

On the above board is another example of a pawn fork. The *black pawn* will capture either the *rook* on **f1** or the *knight* on **h1**.

Bishop Fork,

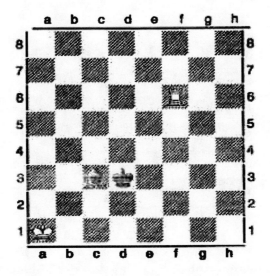

The board above shows that the *bishop* is attacking two pieces at the same time—the rook and the king. This is an example of a *bishop fork*. In this position, the king must move out of check then the bishop will capture the rook.

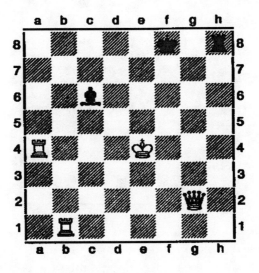

Notice the bishop fork on the rook and king above. The queen will be captured when the king moves.

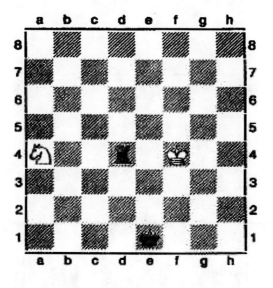

On the board above is a rook fork. Notice that the *rook* is attacking two pieces at the same time—the white king and the white knight. This is an example of a *rook fork*.

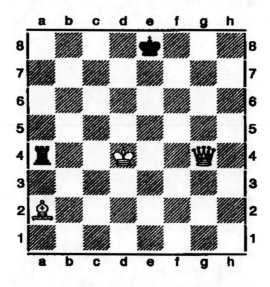

The above board shows another example of a rook fork. Here, the rook is attacking the king and the bishop at the same time. After the king moves out of check, the queen will be captured.

Knight Fork,

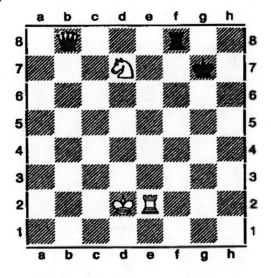

On the board above, the *knight* has forked the queen and the rook. The queen will be captured.

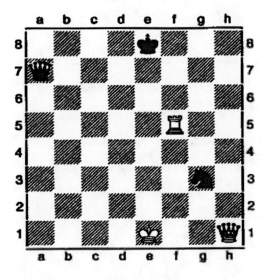

The position that is presented on the above board is another example of a knight fork. The knight is attacking the queen and the rook at the same time. The queen will be captured.

Queen Fork,

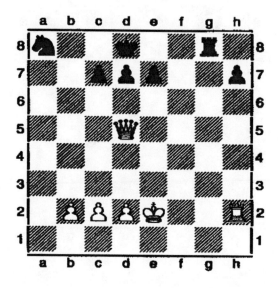

On the board above, the queen is attacking the rook and the knight at the same time. This is an example of a *queen fork.*

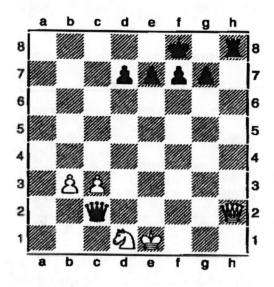

On the board above, the *white queen* has forked the black *rook* and the black *queen.* The best piece to capture would be the *rook* and force a *checkmate.*

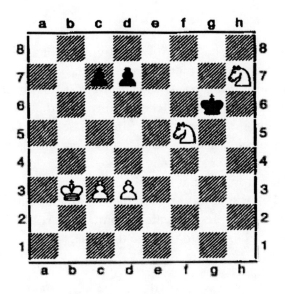

The example on the previous board shows that the *black king* is attacking two knights at the same time. One of the knights will eventually be captured. This example is an example of a *king fork*.

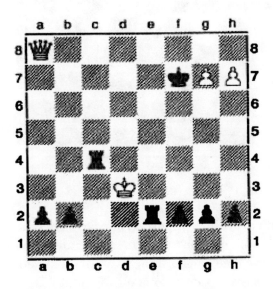

On the above board, the white king is attacking the two black rooks at the same time. This is another example of a *king fork*.

The Pin

The pin is a term used to signify the trapping of a piece in front of a king or in front of another piece. When a piece is pinned in front of the king, it is called an *absolute pin*. When another piece is pinned, it is called a *relative pin*. If an absolute pin is executed, the piece that is standing in front of the king cannot move because the king will be placed in check. With a relative pin, the piece can move, but the opponent will be at a disadvantage in losing a piece after the exchange is made.

It is important to note that only the bishop, rook, and the queen can execute pins. This is so because these pieces can attack at long range. Let us look at some examples of some absolute and relative pins. In these examples, I will call on you to execute these pins.

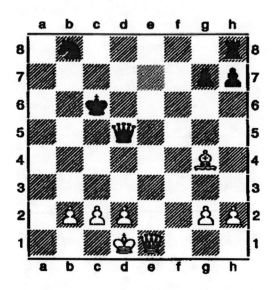

Look carefully at the board above. White has an excellent opportunity to execute a relative pin on black. Do you see the move? If the bishop moves to **f3**, it will pin the queen against the king. Black queen would eventually be captured. This is an example of a bishop pin.

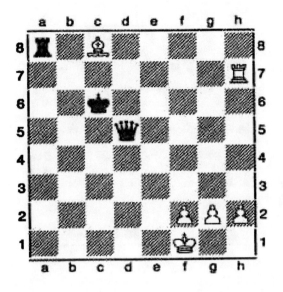

Look at the board above. Black is poised to checkmate white, but it is white's move. What move would you make to capture the black queen? The correct pin is **Bb7** check.

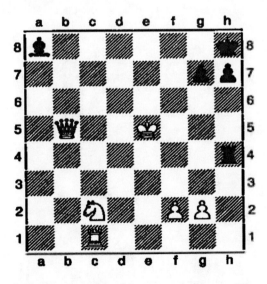

On the board above, it is black's turn to move. The white is getting to checkmate black. What will be the best move for black? Answer: **Rh5,** winning the queen.

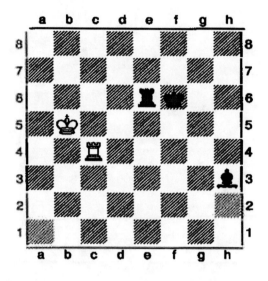

Look at the previous board. The black has a piece advantage. It is white's turn to move. What can white do to force an immediate draw? The white *rook* will move to **c6** forcing an exchange of *rooks*. The bishop alone cannot force a checkmate. This is another example of a relative pin.

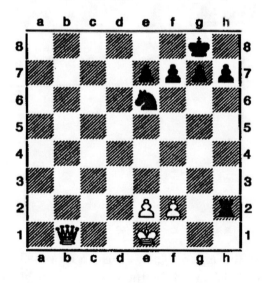

Look at the board above. White is getting ready to checkmate black. It is black's turn to move. Black can use an absolute pin to capture the white queen. Do you see the move? Look, the rook move to **h1**. This is a check. The king must move then the queen will be captured.

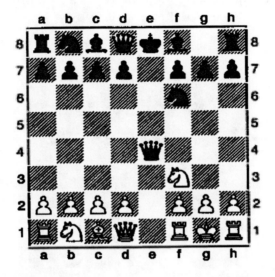

In the above example, the white rook is in a position to pin the queen by moving to **e1**. The black queen will be captured. Do you see the move?

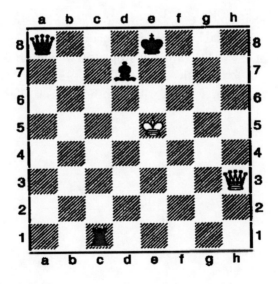

Look at the position on the previous board. It is white's turn to move. Do you see the pin? If the queen moves to **h8**, it will force the king to move out of check then the black queen will be captured.

Breaking the Pin

Many pins are quite serious. Some pins can be broken if the right offensive moves are executed. Let us look at some example how one can break a pin.

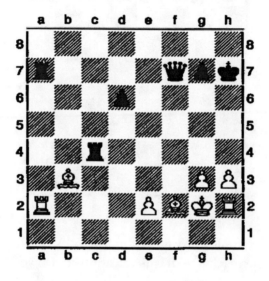

Look at the position on the above board. The white bishop has pinned the rook against the black queen. The black must take an appropriate counter action to break the pin. The appropriate action for black here is black queen moves to **b7** with a check. The white must respond then the black rook is free to move to **c1** with another check. This action breaks the pin.

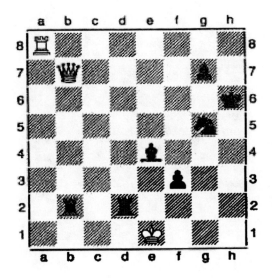

Look closely at the position above. Notice that the black bishop has pinned the white queen against the rook. White now has to find a way to escape. This can be done by moving the rook to **h8** with a check. Black must respond to the check. The white queen can then move to **a6, a7, a8, c7, c8**, or **e7**. The pin is broken.

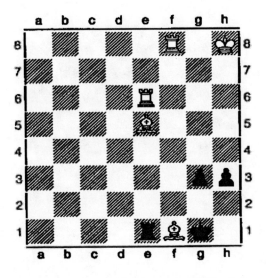

On the board above, the white bishop is pinned. This pin can be broken with **Bd4** then **RxR**. The pin is broken.

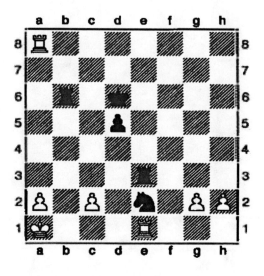

Look at the previous board position. This exercise is tricky. Notice that the white rook has the black knight pinned against the black rook. Black must break this pin. If the black knight moves to **c3**, the logical move for white, for many opponents, is to capture the rook that sits on **e3**. After this capture is made then the rook that sits on **b6** would move to **b1** with a checkmate.

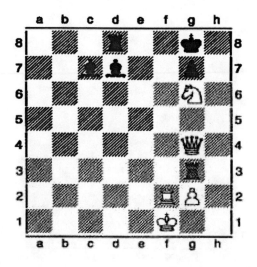

Look at the board above. Notice that the black rook has the white queen pinned against the knight. White must break this pin. Do you see the best move? Knight would move to **e7** with a check. The king can move either to **h8** or **h7**. Queen will then move to **h5** with a checkmate. The pin is broken.

Discovered Check

Discovered check, is a single offensive move that one uses to attack the king and another piece with a single piece. A bishop, queen, rook, and a knight can execute a discovered check. Let us look at some examples.

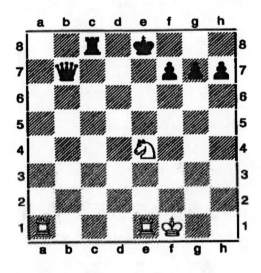

Look at this diagram above. Notice that the white rook and the knight are lined up on the same vertical line. White can execute a discovered check by moving the knight to **c5** or **d6**, attacking the black queen and calling check at the same time. The black queen will eventually be captured.

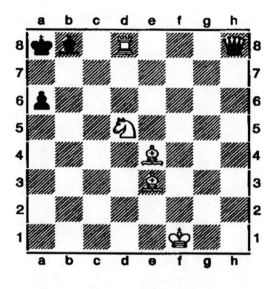

Look at the board above. It is white's turn to move. Do you see the double check? White can move to **c7** with a discovered check and checkmate.

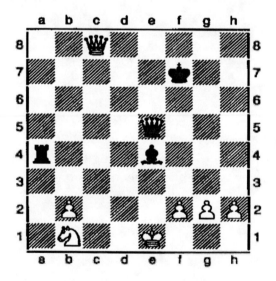

On the previous board position. It is black's turn to move. Bishop would move to **b7** with a check. When the king moves then the bishop will capture the queen.

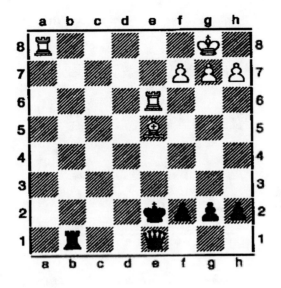

On the previous board, white has a discovered check by moving the bishop to **c3**, forcing the king to move, then the bishop or the rook can capture the queen. This is a very effective double check.

Decoy

The dictionary defines *decoy,* as an act to lead into danger, to lure into a net, to entrap, and to entice. In chess, a tactical strategy is often used to lure a major piece, such as the queen or the king, on a particular square. When that major piece is enticed to that dangerous square then some decisive offensive attacks are executed to ensure the gaining of major pieces or the winning of the game. Let us look at a few examples.

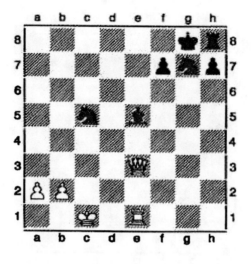

The position on the board above is an excellent example of how the tactical decoy plan can be executed. It is black's turn to move. Do you see the decoy tactic?

Answer: Black would move the bishop to **f4**. The white queen must take. The black knight would then fork the queen on **d3**.

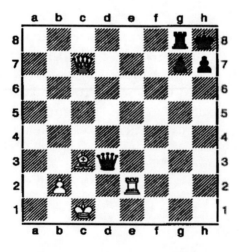

Look at this decoy. It is white's turn to move. Do you see the decoy tactic?

Answer: The white queen would take the pawn on **g7** with a check. The black rook must take the queen. The white rook would then move to **e8** with a checkmate.

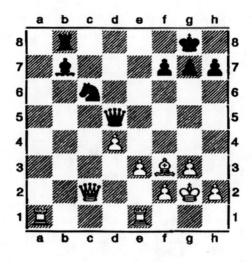

Look carefully at the previous board position. Do you see the decoy for black?

Answer: Black queen captures the bishop on **f3**. The king will capture the queen. Black knight will take the pawn on **d4** with a bishop and a knight check. White is forced to move out of check. The knight then would capture the queen and attacking the two rooks at the same time. Black will win some important pieces in the exchange.

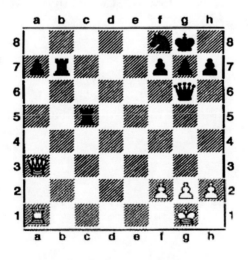

On the board above, the black has the next move. Do you see the decoy?

Answer: The black rook moves to **b1** check. The white rook can capture the black rook then the queen will capture the rook on **b1** with a checkmate. Another option for white is to move the queen on **c1** after the check. That would also lead to a checkmate or the loss of important pieces.

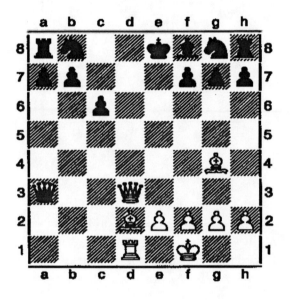

This is a very interesting decoy strategic move. It is white's turn to move. Do you see it?

Answer: The white queen moves to **d8**. The king must take. The bishop would then move to **g5** with a double check. If the king moves to **e8**, the rook would then move to **d8** with a checkmate. If the king moves to **c7** then the bishop would move to **d8** again with a checkmate.

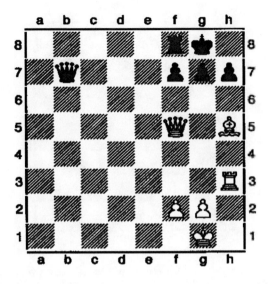

Look at the position on the above board. It is white's turn to move. Do you see the decoy?

Answer: Queen captures the pawn on **h7**. The king is forced to take the queen. The white bishop then captures the **f7** pawn with a checkmate.

What is an Overload?

Many times while playing a game, one would encounter a single overworked chess piece. That single piece is usually forced to guard two pieces at the same time. When such weakness is observed by the attacking player, the correct offensive move must be executed. If the proper offensive move is made, the attacker would win the exchange or a piece by removing the guarded pieces and then capture the other piece that is left unguarded.

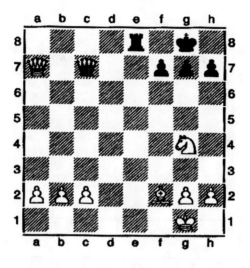

Look at the above move closely. It is black's turn to move. Do you see which piece can be moved from the defending position so that an advantage could be gained?

Answer: Black has an opportunity to capture the white queen. The plan must be executed correctly. First, rook moves to **e1** with a check. This move would draw the bishop away from the defense of the queen. The bishop must take the rook. After this capture, the black queen would capture the white queen. The bishop was overworked.

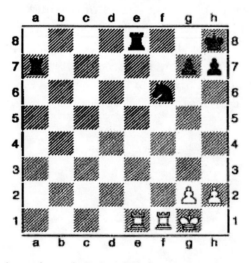

Look at the above board. It is white's turn to move. Do you see the overload? Can white win a major piece and checkmate black?

Answer: The rook on **e1** take **e8**. The knight is forced to take the rook. The rook on **f1** moves to **f8** with a checkmate. The knight was overworked.

On the board below, it is white's turn to move. Do you see how white can remove the overworked piece and gain a piece?

Answer: Queen captures the rook with a check. King captures the queen. White knight moves to **g6**, forking the queen.

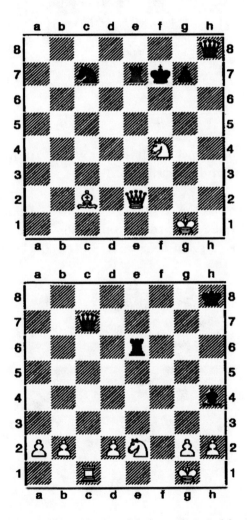

Look at the previous board. On this board, it is black's turn to move. Do you see the overload?

Answer: The queen captures the rook with a check. The knight is forced to capture the queen. Rook then moves to **e1** with a checkmate.

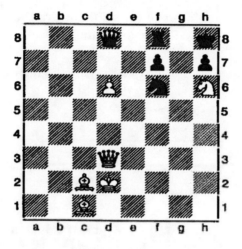

Look at the previous position. It is white's turn to move. Do you see what piece is overworked and how white could gain a major advantage?

Answer: The bishop on **c1** moves to **b2**. This move will pin the knight. Black can now move the queen, the rook, or the king. None of these moves can stop the white queen from moving to **h7** with a checkmate.

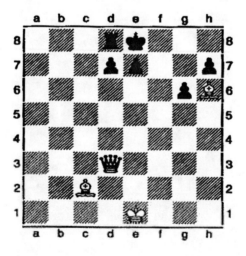

Look at the board above. It is white's turn to move. Do you see the overworked pieces? Do you see how white can take advantage of this weakness?

Answer: Queen would capture the pawn on **g6** The black pawn is forced to capture the queen on **g6**. The bishop would then capture the pawn on **g6** with a checkmate.

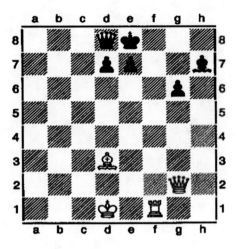

Look at the board above. It is white's turn to move. Do you see the overworked piece?

Answer: Queen captures the pawn on **g6** with a check. Bishop captures the queen. Bishop captures the bishop with a checkmate.

What is a Deflection?

In many team sports, a decoy or a distraction is used to prevent the opposing team from focusing. In chess, the tactic of deflection, is used to distract a guard and chase it away from defending an important piece. After the guard leaves from that defensive position, the defending piece is then left unprotected and will be captured. Let us review some of these examples:

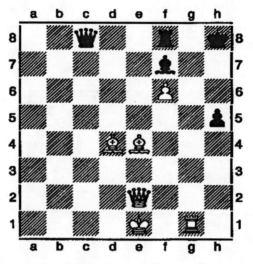

Look at the board above. It is white's turn to move. The queen would capture the pawn on **h5** with a check. Black has no other choice but to capture the queen. The white pawn will then move to **f7** with a checkmate. An excellent deflective move.

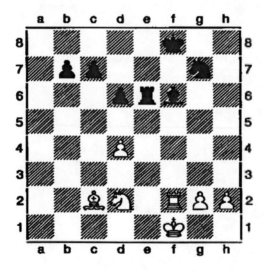

Look at the board above. It is white's turn to move. Do you see how white can gain a piece by using a deflection move?

Answer: White moves to **d5**, attacking the rook. The rook is forced to respond. The rook can only move vertically away from the bishop. The bishop is then captured.

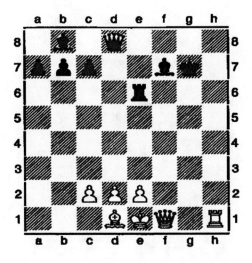

The position above is very interesting. It is white's turn to move. Do you see the deflection move?

Answer: White rook moves to **h7**. This move forces the king to capture the rook or move to **g8**, **g6**, or **f8**. If the king captures the rook, the white queen will capture the black bishop with a check, and then the rook will fall. If the king moves to any other square, the queen will also capture the bishop on **f7** then the rook or possible checkmate on **h7**.

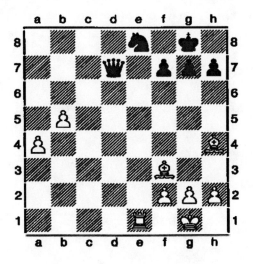

White is to move on the above board. What is the best move? Answer: White bishop moves to **c6**.

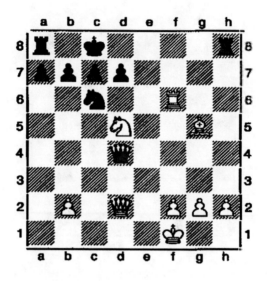

Another interesting position exists on the board above. It is white's turn to move. Do you see the best deflective move?

Answer: White would like to win the queen, but it is guarded by the black knight. The best plan therefore is to call a check on **e7** with the knight. With this check, the knight is drawn away from protecting the queen. Black has only three choices. To capture the knight with the knight, move the king to **b8**, or move the king to **d8**. With either of the king's moves, the knight will move from that position on **c6** with another check. The queen is then left unguarded. The queen will then be captured by the white queen.

Summary questions

Answer the following questions by circling the word *never, sometimes,* or *always.* The expectation level is 80 percent correct.

1. When a castle is executed, the rook must move first.
    a. Always   b. Sometimes   c. Never

2. One can castle through the line of check
    a. Always   b. Sometimes   c. Never

3. The term *check* means that the king cannot move.
    a. Always   b. Sometimes   c. Never

4. The queen can be placed in check sometimes.
    a. Always   b. Sometimes   c. Never

5. A fork can only be executed by a queen and a knight.
    a. Always   b. Sometimes   c. Never

6. A king can capture another king
    a. Always   b. Sometimes   c. Never

7. The kingside and the queenside of a chessboard is similar.
    a. Always   b. Sometimes   c. Never

8. In many instances, a game could continue if the king leaves the chessboard.
    a. Always   b. Sometimes   c. Never

9. The symbol # means checkmate.
    a. Always   b. Sometimes   c. Never

10. The symbol **0-0-0** means castling on the king side.
    a. Always   b. Sometimes   c. Never

11. The symbol ½-½ mean that the game is a draw.
    a. Always   b. Sometimes   c. Never

12. The symbol **1-0** means that white has won the game.
    a. Always   b. Sometimes   c. Never

13. A rook and a king alone can checkmate an opponent.
    a. Always   b. Sometimes   c. Never

14. A bishop and a king alone can checkmate an opponent.
    a. Always   b. Sometimes   c. Never

15. A knight and a king alone can checkmate an opponent.
    a. Always   b. Sometimes   c. Never

16. A queen alone can checkmate an opponent without the help from any other piece.
    a. Always   b. Sometimes   c. Never

17. The notation **e4** means that a pawn is on the fourth file.
    a. always   b. Sometimes   c. Never

18. The pieces that have a long range attack are the knights, pawns, and kings.
    a. Always   b. Sometimes   c. Never

19. A stalemate is a draw, but the game could continue.
    a. Always   b. Sometimes   c. Never

20. When a pin is executed, the opponent will always lose a piece.
    a. Always   b. Sometime   c. Never

21. All chess pieces can execute a pin.
    a. Always   b. Sometimes   c. Never

22. All chess pieces can execute a fork.
    a. Always   b. Sometimes   c. Never

23. When a double check is executed, one of the pieces that is under attack must be the king.
    a. Always   b. Sometimes   c. Never

24. The algebraic must be used when recording a chess.
    a. Always   b. Sometimes   c. Never

25. En passant means that a game is finished.
    a. Always   b. Sometimes   c. Never

Answers to questions:

1. *Never*   One cannot castle while the king is in check.
2. *Never*   One cannot castle through check.
3. *Never*   It means that the king is under attack.
4. *Never*   The queen can never be placed in check.
5. *Sometimes*   A fork can be executed by all of the pieces.
6. *Never*   A king can never capture another king.
7. *Never*   Both sides are different.
8. *Never*   The king remains on the board.
9. *Always*   # is the notation for checkmate.
10. *Never*   0-0-0 means castling on the queen side.
11. *Always*   ½ means the game ends in a draw.
12. *Always*   1-0 means that white has won the game.
13. *Always*   A rook and a king are mating material.
14. *Never*   Not enough mating material with just the bishop alone.
15. *Never*   Not enough mating material.
16. *Never*   A queen alone cannot mate someone without the help from another piece.
17. *Never*   The piece is on the 4th rank.
18. *Never*   The queen, bishop and the rook have long range attack.
19. *Never*   A stalemate is a draw. The game ends.
20. *Sometimes* A pin can be broken sometimes.
21. *Never*   A queen, rook, and a bishop can execute pins.
22. *Always*   All pieces can execute a fork.
23. *Always*   One of the pieces must be the king.
24. *Sometimes* Other notations can be used. Algebraic is only one of many.
25. *Never*   En passant means pawn in passing.

Chapter 10

In this chapter, we will continue to review some of the basic chess terms and positions a player should become familiar with:

Double Check

Double check, is almost similar to a discovered check. This is another offensive tactical move that places a double check on the enemy king. With a discovered check, the king and another piece are under attack. With a double check, the enemy king is checked twice by two attacking pieces. Let us look at some examples:

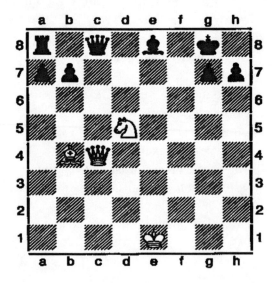

Look closely at the board above. White is to move. Do you see the double check? White knight used an attacking move by playing **Ne7** with a check. The knight is attacking the king and the black queen at the same time. Also, with that move, the white queen also has the king in check. The king must move, and the knight will then capture the queen.

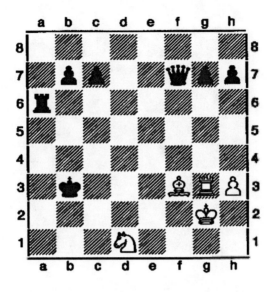

White has an excellent double check by attacking the queen with a move to **d5** with the bishop and checking the king with the rook. The queen will be captured.

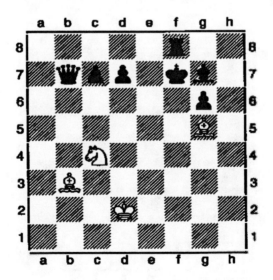

Take a close look at the board above. White is to move. Do you see the double check? Black has overwhelming pieces, but look at what occurs. Knight moves to **d6** with a double check. King cannot move. That is checkmate.

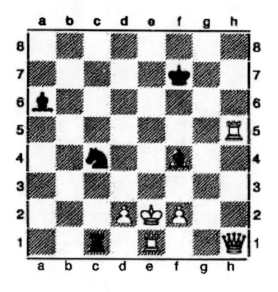

Look closely at the board above. It is black's turn to move. Note that white is getting ready to crush black. Black has found a way out. Do you see the double check and checkmate? Black knight captures the pawn on **d2**. Rook will block then **BxR** with a checkmate.

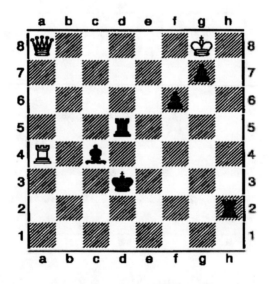

Look at the board above. It is black's turn to move. Do you see the double check? Rook moves to **d8** with a double check and checkmate.

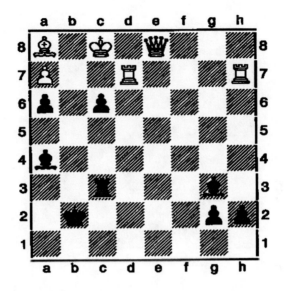

Look at this last example of a double check. On the above board, it is black's turn to move. Notice that white has more valuable pieces, but black pieces are better placed. Do you see the double check? Pawn captures the rook on **d7;** the king must move to **d8.** The pawn then captures the queen on **e8** with a checkmate.

The Skewer

The skewer is a member of the pin family. Just like the pin, it is a single move with a single piece attacking two pieces with one move. Usually it is one important piece and a piece of less importance. Quite often, the most important piece is in front of the lesser valued piece. In the case of a king and the queen, this is very effective. Usually the enemy king is in front of its queen. Sometimes there are skewers that are executed on pieces with the same value. The piece in the back will most likely be captured. Let us look at some examples of the skewer:

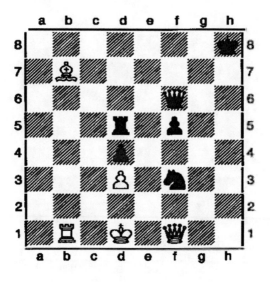

Look at the diagram above. Do you see the skewer? The white bishop has attacked the rook and the knight. One of these pieces will be captured.

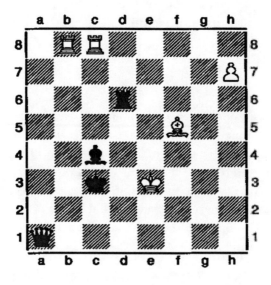

Look at this skewer. Black has the temporary advantage, but it is white's turn to move. White will advance the pawn to **h8** and ask for a queen. This queen will check the king. The black queen will eventually be captured with a checkmate in sight.

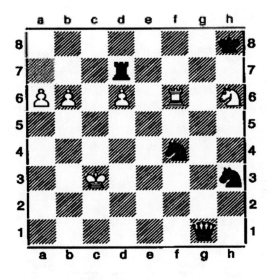

This is another skewer. Black's turn to move. Do you see how black could capture a major piece by employing the skewer? If the queen moves to **a1**, that would be a check. The white king must move out of check then the rook will be captured.

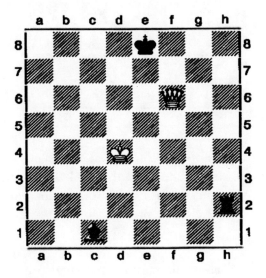

On the previous board is an example of a simple skewer. It is black's turn to move. Black bishop would move to **b2** with a check. The white king must move then the queen is captured.

Removing the Guard

Sometimes an attack is launched on your opponent's piece or the king, but another piece is standing in the way, preventing the attacker from executing the move. Sometimes it is a pawn, bishop, knight, rook, or a queen, guarding another piece or the king. When this occurs, the attacker must decide if the guard should be moved to take advantage of the position. What would happen if the guard is captured? Would this compromise the effect of the attacking forces or would this give the attacking force the big prize?

Let us look at some of these positions:

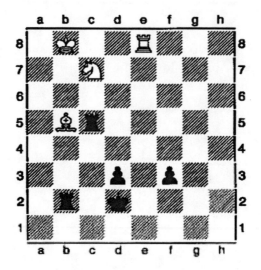

Look at the board above. Notice that white has three remaining pieces—the bishop, the knight, and the rook. The knight is guarding the bishop. The main question for black is how can two of the pieces be exchanged for one of the black pieces? Do you see how the guard can be moved?

Answer: The rook on c5 would capture the knight then the rook on b2 would capture the bishop.

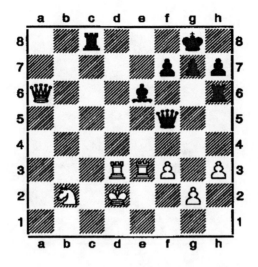

Look at the position on the board above. It is white's turn to move. Notice that the bishop is guarding the rook that sits on **c8**. Do you see how the guard can be removed?

Answer: Queen captures the rook that sits on **c8** with a check. The bishop must capture. Rook now moves to **d8** with a checkmate.

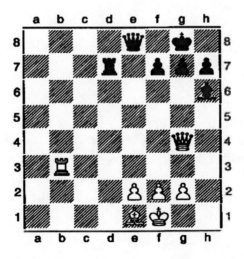

On the board above, white is to move. Do you see how to move the guard? Note: **QxR** then black queen takes queen followed with **Rb8**. This will force a mate.

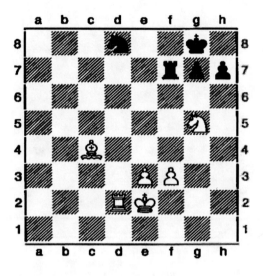

Look at the previous board. It is white's turn to move. White is in a position to win a piece and checkmate.

Answer: Knight captures the knight on **d8**. That is a checkmate. The rook is pinned.

Offering A Draw

When a game cannot be won by either side, it is called a draw. A draw can be obtained by the following methods:

1. If both players agree for a draw A draw can be offered to an opponent on the first move. A player can refuse to accept a draw at any point in a game. When a draw if offered, one should ask, "Would you like, or accept, a draw?" It is always courteous to respond to such request, either as "No, I will think about it" or "The draw is accepted." It is never proper to continue asking an opponent

for draw after every move. It is also not proper for an opponent not to respond to the opponent for a draw continuously especially when checkmate is obvious in a few moves. It is not proper chess courtesy.

2. If the game ends in a stalemate Remember, a stalemate is when a king is placed in a position where it cannot move on any open square. If the king moves, it would be moving on an illegal square.

3. Three-move repetition If both black and white move in the same position three times consistently, that action is considered as a draw. This especially occurs when an opponent continues to check the king, and that king continues to move back and forth on the same squares, with the same moves, three times. It is obvious that if these moves do not end, they can continue forever.

4. Moving fifty moves without moving a pawn or without capturing another piece A chess game cannot continue forever. It must end sometime. Fifty moves without capturing a piece or moving a pawn is enough to end a game. This fifty moves should be counted on both sides—fifty moves for black and fifty moves for white. If a pawn or a piece is captured within the fifty-move count, then both parties must start again, starting back to move one.

5. If there are not enough pieces on the board to checkmate the opponent If a player has only a bishop and a king, and the opponent has just the king on the board, that game is a definite draw. The same applies to a knight alone with a king. Interestingly, a pawn has less value than a bishop and a knight, but a pawn alone on the board with a king can advance to the eighth or the first ranks and be promoted to a queen or a rook. Both the promoted queen or the rook can hen launch an attack on the king and execute a checkmate. The pawn by itself will not force a checkmate on the opponent king without being promoted to another piece.

Let us look at a few examples of how someone can force a draw.

How to Force a Draw

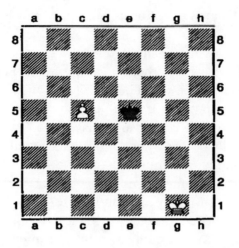

On the board above, it appears that the pawn will advance for a queen. If black makes a wrong move then the game will be won by white. It is white's turn to move. Do you see the draw?

Answer: If the pawn moves to **c6** then the king will move to **d6**. If any other move is made then the king will move to **d5**. The main objective is to capture the advancing pawn.

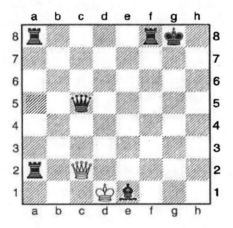

On the board above, black has the advantage. White must try to draw this game. Do you see the draw?

Answer: **Qg6** then to **h6** with perpetual checks.

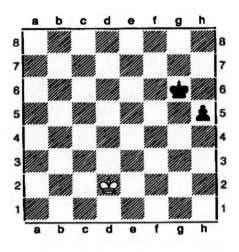

Look closely at the position on the previous board. It is black's turn to move. Do you see the draw?

Answer: The white king must travel and get to **g2** before the pawn can advance to **h1**. This is a draw.

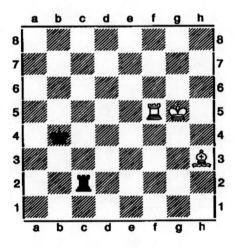

Look at the previous board. White has the advantage, and black must force a draw. Do you see the draw?

Answer: Black rook moves to **c5**, forcing a rook exchange. The bishop and the king alone cannot force a win.

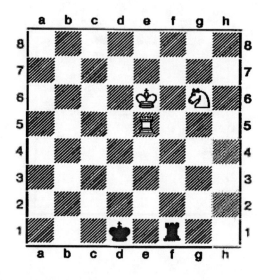

It is black's turn to move and can force a draw. Do you see the forced draw? Answer: **Re1** forcing the rook exchange. The knight alone cannot win.

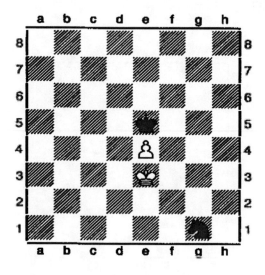

On the board above, it is black's turn to move. Do you see the draw? Answer: **Nh3** then **Ng5** then **Ne4**.

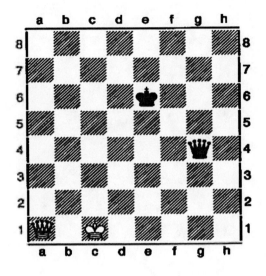

The above position is recognized as a draw.

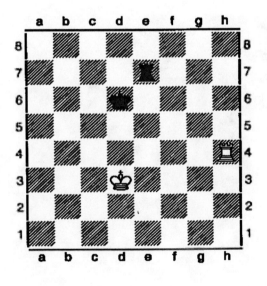

The position above is recognized as a draw.

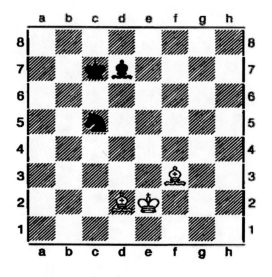

The position above is recognized as a draw.

Chapter 11

How Best to Open

Successful chess players always plan their games before they actually sit behind the chessboard. Very often, such players think about their openings, their center games, and their end games before the actual game starts. The opening game is generally the first ten moves. These moves are critical because they dictate what will happen in the middle and the end game. The following basic opening principles should be used to develop and improve one chess game:

1. Maintain control of the center with proper pawn movement. What is the center game? The idea of the center game is to control the center four squares. Those center squares are, **e4**, **d4**, **e5**, and **d5**. If pawns occupy these squares then it becomes easier to launch further attacks. These four pawns control the outcome of the chess game.

2. Develop your pieces early. Avoid moving the same pawn and other pieces three, four, and more times in the opening. If an opponent is attacking, ask yourself the question, Should the victim just stand with his or her hands tied behind the back and expect to win? The victim will never win such a battle. If one is looking for a victory in chess, rapid development of all pieces is advisable. One cannot win chess battles with poor development. The valuable pieces must leave the back rank and work in unison with other pieces while executing an attack.

3. Castle early. Get your king out of danger by the fifth to the seventh move. If one king is exposed to an opponent's attacking pieces, it will be captured. If a king is protected, one can then concentrate on how to launch attacks with the other pieces and win more games.

Castling allows the king to be protected from all dangers and at the same time activates the rook into an attacking position.

4.   Develop your minor pieces first, then your major pieces last. Control the center with your pawns then develop the knights and the bishops. Move the knights, the bishops, and other pieces toward the center of the board. It is important not to block the escape vents for your minor and major pieces. The diagonal files should not be blocked with pawns. This will hinder the development of the bishops. The rook functions better in open files. Try to connect those rooks and not block their escape route with pawns.

5.   Avoid exposing your queen too early. When a queen is brought out early in a game, it stands the chance of being captured by an experienced opponent. That opponent will use the opportunity to launch an attack on the queen by closing off all of its escape routes. A queen that is lost early in the game without reasonable compensation could mean a weaker defense and offense and an early defeat.

6.   Avoid hanging pieces Putting an attacking piece on an open file without the support from other pieces could mean that the piece will be captured and both the defense and offense will be affected. When a major piece is captured in the opening game, one is forced to regroup and possibly shift to a defending mode. Losing an early piece, without the necessary compensation, will change the tone and the outcome of the game.

7.   Do not waste time to develop important pieces. It is always recommended to open with the center pawns then the knight, bishop, and then castle. One cannot waste time developing important pieces. If a piece is moved twice in the opening, the move advantage is then shifted to the opponent. All little advantages in chess are advantage gained. White has the first advantage by moving first. Moving a bishop, pawn, or a knight twice in the opening game actually turns the move advantage over to black.

Using the Clock

Chess clocks are instruments that are used to time chess games. Most tournament games are usually timed. A time clock is comprised of two separate clocks under one casing. Each clock has its individual button. These buttons are used to stop and activate each clock.

At the beginning of a timed game, both parties or the arbitrators would indicate how long a particular game would last. If the time period is one hour per player, then the clock would be set for sixty minutes on each clock. The person with the white pieces would move first then the button on top of the clock nearest to the player would be pushed. The person who is playing black always hits the clock first.

It is important to note that the clock should be placed on the right-hand side of the person who is playing black.

It is proper to hit the clock or push the button with the same hand that is used to move the pieces. Both players would move and hit the clock alternately. If a player's flag drops or the time ends, the game would be stopped. If both players have *mating* materials, a win will be awarded to the player who has time left on the clock. If a flag is down or the time runs out for a player, the arbitrator would check the board to see if the player whose clock is still running has mating material. If that player has insufficient mating material, such as a bishop and a king only, or a knight and a king, then the game would be declared a draw.

Summary Questions:

Answer the questions by placing a circle around *always, sometimes,* or *never.* Each question values four points. The answers for these questions can be found on the previous page.

1. When the king is double checked, the king has no escape squares to move, and it is checkmated.
    a. Always   b. Sometimes   c. Never

2. A double check can be executed with a bishop and a knight or a rook and a queen working together.
    a. Always   b. Sometimes   c. Never

3. Three consecutive repetitive moves is a draw
    a. Always   b. Sometimes   c. Never

4. If a player move a piece or pieces twenty-five moves as long as there is no pawn captured or moved this is considered to be a draw.
    a. Always   b. Sometimes   c. Never

5. A stalemate can be considered a draw.
   a. Always   b. Sometimes   c. Never

6. A person who has insufficient mating material can still win the game.
   a. Always   b. Sometimes   c. Never

7. If both parties have just a bishop and a king alone on the chessboard, the game is a draw.
   a. Always   b. Sometimes   c. Never

8. A rook and a king against the opponent king alone is a clear draw.
   a. Always   b. Sometimes   c. Never

9. Two kings alone on the chessboard is a draw
   a. Always   b. Sometimes   c. Never

10. A king and a pawn against a king alone could be a win.
    a. Always   b. Sometimes   c. Never

11. Both players usually receive one point for each game that is drawn.
    a. Always   b. Sometimes   c. Never

12. A person can never recover from a poor open move.
    a. Always   b. Sometimes   c. Never

13. A knight can move an L pattern but can never capture a piece backward.
    a. Always   b. Sometimes   c. Never

14. The knight is the only chess piece that can jump over other pieces.
    a. Always   b. Sometimes   c. Never

15. It is possible for a person to have as many as nine queens on the board.
    a. Always   b. Sometimes   c. Never

16. It is always important for a player to maintain control of the middle of the chessboard during the opening moves.
    a. Always   b. Sometimes   c. Never

17. When a castle is executed, one of the rooks must move on that specific move.

    a. Always   b. Sometimes   c. Never

18. Clocks can only be used in tournament

    a. Always   b. Sometimes   c. Never

19. A player must hit the clock with the same hand that is used to move the pieces.

    a. Always   b. Sometimes   c. Never

20. Chess games are not timed for less than one hour per game

    a. Always   b. Sometimes   c. Never

21. Fumbling an opponent pieces is allowed as long as the piece is not removed from the board.

    a. Always   b. Sometimes   c. Never

22. A queen and a king against a king is considered to be insufficient mating material.

    a. Always   b. Sometimes   c. Never

23. In chess, it is always better to take a draw than a loss.

    a. Always   b. Sometimes   c. Never

24. A fork can only be executed with a knight.

    a. Always   b. Sometimes   c. Never

25. A queen can checkmate another queen.

    a. Always   b. Sometimes   c. Never

Answers to Questions

1. *Sometimes*   Double check does not mean that the game is finished. On some occasions the king is checkmated and on other occasions the king can move to other legal squares.

2. *Sometimes*   A double check can be executed with all of the pieces working together with another piece.

3. *Always*   Three repetitive moves is a draw. This is one of the basic chess rules.
4. *Never*   The rule states that each player must make fifty moves and not twenty five.
5. *Always*   A stalemate is always a draw.
6. *Never*   Insufficient material means that the person does not have enough pieces to execute a mate.
7. *Always*   This is an example of insufficient material. The bishop and a king, without the help of other offensive or defensive pieces, cannot force a checkmate.
8. *Sometimes*   In most cases, a rook and a king can checkmate an opponent king. However, if the opponent blunders, a draw can be achieved.
9. *Always*   One king cannot checkmate another king.
10. *Sometimes*   A pawn and a king can win against a king alone. It depends on the position of the opposing king. On many occasion, this turns out to be a draw.
11. *Never*   When a game is drawn, both players receive one half of a point.
12. *Sometimes*   One can lose many games with a series of poor openings. However, one can also recover and finish with a strong middle and end game.
13. *Never*   A knight can always capture a piece backward.
14. *Always*   No other chess piece is allowed to jump over other pieces on the chessboard.
15. *Always*   This is possible, but it seldom happens.
16. *Always*   This is very important. Controlling the middle of the game does dictate the movement of the other pieces.
17. *Always*   Only one rook is allowed to move when a single castle is executed.
18. *Sometimes*   Clock can also be used when two people are playing a casual and friendly game.
19. *Always*   This is the rule of the game. The player must use the same hand that is used to move the pieces to hit the clock.
20. *Sometimes*   A game can be timed for any agreed minutes. A tournament game is usually 60 or 90 minutes per person. A game however, can be played for thirty, twenty, ten, or less minutes.
21. *Never*   Fumbling an opponent's pieces is not an acceptable practice. It is disrespectful to one's opponent.

22. *Never*   The queen and a king versus a king is mating material. One can surely execute checkmate with these two pieces.
23. *Always*   A half of a point is better than no point.
24. *Sometimes*   A fork can be executed with all of the pieces. Most of the time, a knight is usually mentioned.
25. *Never*   A queen can never be checkmated., only the king.

Chapter 12

Chess Etiquette

There are rules and expectations that every chess player should adhere to. Respect for the game and respect for one's opponent are paramount. Let us examine some of these basic concerns.

1. Choosing a Color

    I have witnessed much confusion as to which player should play what color. Some individuals love to play the white pieces and others love to play black. The method that is selected must give each player a fifty-fifty chance of selecting one of the colors.

2. Sitting Behind the Chessboard

    Sitting directly behind the chessboard gives a new player a better vision of the board, pieces, and possible mates. Further, if the game is being timed and scored, the player will get a better view of the clock and the score sheet. It is quite annoying if a player plays the game from the side of the board and impedes on the opponent's space. After the color is selected, then the person who is playing black should sit directly behind the black queen and king. These two pieces are located in the center of the playing side. The same position is also true for the person who has selected white. That person should sit directly behind the white queen and king.

3. Talking the Game

    Nothing can be more annoying than having someone, including an opponent, telling a player what piece or pieces to move in a chess game. The person should be allowed to think, and then after the game, a review of the moves can be initiated. Just imagine how the frustration can be built up if your opponent continue to comment every time you move a piece. Imagine your opponent or his friends saying to you that your move is inferior. It is important to remember that the golden rule must be followed. Each player should do unto each other how they expect to be treated. All players and friends should remain quiet during the game.

4. Distracting Your Opponent

Some people use different ploys to upset their opponents. When these annoyances are allowed in a game, it gives the advantage to the person who is creating the problems. Radios, cell phones, walkman, tapping on the table, continuous coughing and sneezing, combing of hair, smoking, and other distractions are not permitted while engaging in a chess game. Recognizing and respecting your opponent's space around the table is one of the basic principles of the game of chess.

5. Shaking of Hands

Shaking of hands before and after the game should be practiced by all chess players. Basic respect for an opponent is more important than the game itself. A chess game will last for a few minutes or hours, but attitudes and friendships last a lifetime. It is an acceptable practice to shake hands at the beginning of the game and say good luck and at the end of the game to say, good game.

6. Abusive Remarks

Complete respect for the principles of the game and all players should be practiced at all times. When someone loses a game of chess, name calling, the use of foul language, and negative attitude should not be introduced as an excuse for the loss.

7. Touch Move

One of the rules of chess states that once a piece is touched, it must be moved. One cannot use the excuse that the piece was slightly touched or the piece was not intended to be touched.

The only exception to this rule is when a piece is being adjusted on a square. In this case, the person who is making sure that the piece is placed properly on a given square, must say "adjust" while holding the piece in question. Once the word "adjust" is announced, an opponent cannot be forced to move the piece in question. It is important to note that a piece cannot be moved, released, held again, and then call adjust.

8. Touch Take
    One cannot touch or fumble an opponent's pieces. An opponent's pieces cannot be captured, placed back on the board, announce that you are sorry, and then capture a more valuable piece. This practice is unacceptable and illegal. Each player is responsible for touching and adjusting his own pieces.

9. Playing for the Next Player
    Some players have a habit of telling their opponents what pieces they should move during an ongoing game. Some would even make comments such as, "That is an inferior move" or "You should have made another move." This action is a subtle disrespect to an opponent. Players should reserve comments about a game that is ongoing unless both players agree before the game starts that this action would be accepted. Nothing is wrong with making comments or even review of a game after the game is played. Each player should be responsible for his own moves and mistakes during a game without being bombarded with comments and insults.

10. Ridiculing Your Opponent
    Some people have a habit of calling their opponent dirty names especially when they notice that they are at a disadvantage and are about to lose a game. It is often said that the true test of a person is not how he performs as a winner but the attitude that is demonstrated when the "chips are down" or when a game is lost. Occasionally, I have witnessed angry outbursts displayed when an individual loses a game. Some persons call their opponents dirty

names. Some turn over the chessboard, and others find comfort in the use of profanity. The game of chess is the oldest game in the world, and all of the rules of this game must be respected. The followers of the game expect to be associated with a family of friends who can think, reason, analyze, demonstrate respect for others, be graceful, and courteous. The displaying of a negative attitude toward the game is a form of disrespect to all of the players who have made chess the most popular game in the world. Any negative attitude should never be tolerated in any sport and especially the game of chess.

11. Moving the Chessboard

Some people have a natural habit of holding and pulling the chessboard while they are playing a game. This practice can wear down an opponent's patience. It is distracting. It forces one to lose concentration and eventually the game. Players are encouraged to fold or sit on their hands to avoid this practice. In tournament games, an arbitrator can disqualify a player if this habit is demonstrated. The only time the board should be touched is when the pieces are being placed on the board at the beginning of the game or when the pieces are moved from one square to the next during a game.

12. Using the Correct Hand

The same hand that is used to move the pieces should be used to hit the clock and also to write the moves down. One should not use one's right hand to move a piece, and the left to write down the move, and then the right again to hit the clock. This practice is not legal in chess.

13. Leaning on the Board

Leaning on or over the chessboard should not be practiced. Each player must be given enough acceptable space to view all of the pieces that are placed on the board. Each player should exercise control of their designated side and not the entire board. A chess player should never be intimidated by an opponent. Dominance in a game of chess refers to a specific position of the pieces on the board not the physical controlling presence of a player.

14. Placing your hand over the chessboard

Holding on to a piece and hanging it over the chessboard for seconds before placing it on a given square is an unacceptable practice. It is a difficult task for some people to think, then pick up a desired piece, then move that piece to an expected square. Respect your opponent's space over the chessboard.

15. Hitting your Clock

Clock should be hit only to be activated and deactivated. It should never be hit to become disabled. I have seen some clocks used in one game and become so abused that they had to be discarded. Clocks are important tools of chess games. These instruments should be handled with care and patience. Hitting the clock with the right hand and with the appropriate force is an acceptable practice of the game. This art should be learned and practice.

16. Signing your Score Sheet

Many chess games are played and are not recorded. Score sheets that are used to record official games should always be signed by both players after the game is completed. Before the score sheet is submitted to the arbitrator, each score sheet must have two signatures. This is a verification that the game was played and the outcome was agreed upon by both parties. It is advisable that both parties collect a copy of each recorded game for future reference.

17. Slamming the Pieces

Chess pieces are not domino pieces and should not be treated like dominoes. Slamming chess pieces on the chessboard would break the pieces, damage the chessboard, intimidate an opponent, distract other players, and will foster unacceptable habits in youngsters and first-time players. All chess pieces can be lifted and moved to their desired square without making a sound. The quality and the integrity of the game is never compromised by moving quietly.

FIDE: Article 4.1

Each move must be made with one hand only.

FIDE: Article 4.3

If the player who is moving a piece, deliberately touches . . . (a) one or more of his own pieces, he must move the first piece that was touched, as long as that piece can legally move. Also, if a player touches one or more of his opponent's pieces, he must capture the first piece touched as long as that piece can legally be captured.

Chapter 13

Defense against Checkmate

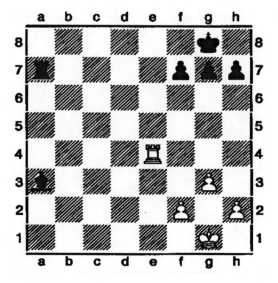

S ometimes it appears as though the game is over. Before such assumption is made, it is important that the defensive move for the opponent be examined carefully. Let us look at the board above. It seems that white will checkmate black if the rook moves from **e4** to **e8**. But wait, if black moves the bishop to **f8**, mate is averted.

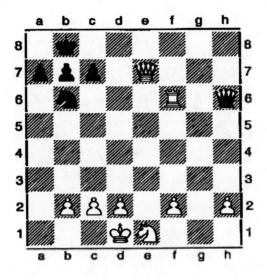

On the board above, it appears as though black is checkmated if the white queen moves to **d8**. But wait, if the black knight moves to **c8**, mate will be averted.

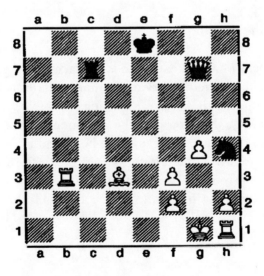

Look at the board above. It is black's turn to move. Black thinks that white is checkmated if the rook moves to **c1**. But wait, if the rook moves to **c1** then the white bishop would move to **f1**.

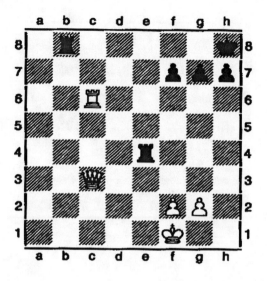

Look at the board above. Is black checkmated? No! White moves the rook to **c8** with a check. If the black rook takes the rook, black would be a checkmated. If the other rook moves from **e4** to **e8**, the checkmate would be averted.

Visualizing Checkmate

The main focus of any chess game is to place the opponent king in a position to be checkmated. Every move that is made by both player is a step closer to achieving that goal. Visualizing checkmate is critical. A good chess player is always thinking how the opponent can be checkmated in the least amount of moves. If a game can be ended in one, two, or three moves, end it. If your opponent is given a chance to recover, he or she will take advantage of a recovered position and would most likely win the game. Let us examine some obvious mates. Can you visualize these mates?

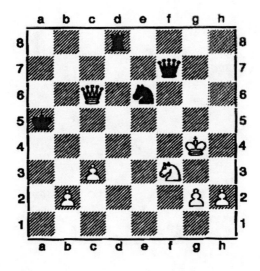

Examine the above board carefully. What is the best move for white? Look, carefully. If the white's pawn moves to **b4,** the king will have no escape route. That will be a *checkmate.*

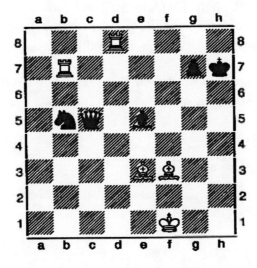

On the board above, it is white turn's to move. What is the best move for white? Answer: **Be4**. Mate!

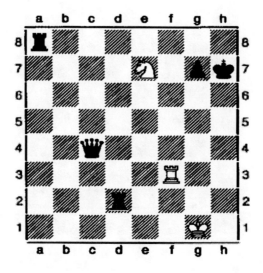

Do you see the best move for white on the above board? Answer **Rh3** will force a mate!

Look closely at the last two boards on the previous page. Do you see checkmate for black on the first board? If rook moves to any square on the *second* rank, it will be a checkmate. Do you see checkmate on the second board? If pawn moves to **c3,** that will be a checkmate.

Look at the board above. It is white's time to move. What is the best move for white? Knight moves to **b6**. That is checkmate.

Examine the above board carefully. Do you see the best move for black? Pawn moves to **c2**. That is a checkmate!

Look at the board above. It is white's turn to move. Do you see the best move? Knight moves to **h6**, and that is checkmate!

Look at the above board. It is black's turn to move. What is the best move for black? Rook moves to **a1**. That is checkmate!

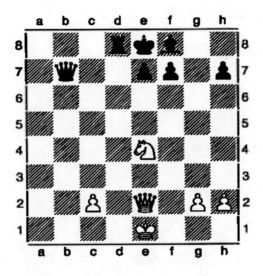

Let us carefully look at the above board. What is white's best move? Look, **e4** to **f6**, checkmate.

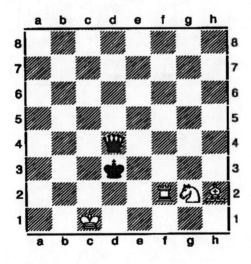

Look at the board above. What is the best move for black? Do you see the move? Queen moves to **a1**. That is a checkmate!

Combinations

Part of the beauty of chess is to vision checkmate in two, three, or more moves. When your pieces are strategically placed, you can mentally announce checkmate by forcing your opponent to respond exactly to your well-thought-out plan. Here are a few well-executed plans that have left black with very little options. White is forcing checkmate in two moves. Can you see these checkmates?

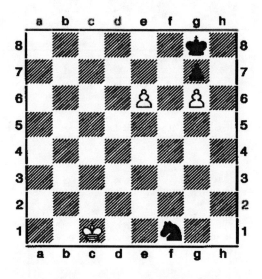

Look at the combination above. It is white's turn to move. White will checkmate black in two moves. The pawn will move to **e7** and then to **e8**. That is checkmate in two moves.

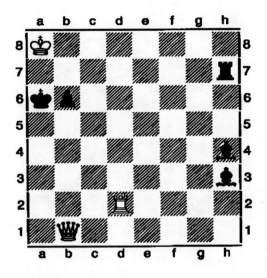

Look at this move above. Do you see checkmate? It is black's turn to move. Rook will move to **a7** with a check then bishop moves to **g3** with a checkmate. Also, **Rh8** with a check, **Rd8** followed with **RxR** mate.

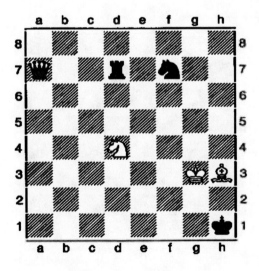

On the board above, white can execute mate in two moves. Do you see the checkmate? Answer: **Bg2** then **Ne2**.

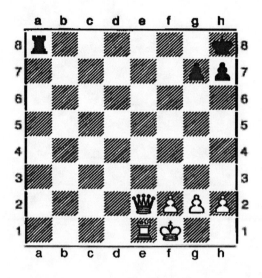

Look at the board above. It is white's turn to move. Do you see the combination and checkmate? Queen moves to **e8** with a check. Rook captures the queen. The white rook now captures the rook with a checkmate.

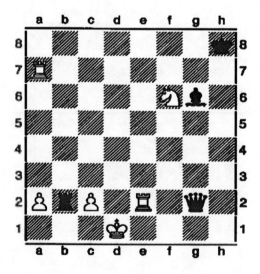

Here is another beautiful combination. Do you see the checkmate? White is to move. Look carefully. Note that the guard must be moved first before checkmate can be executed. Look, rook moves to **e8**, forcing the bishop to capture it, then the rook on **a7** moves to **h7** with a checkmate!

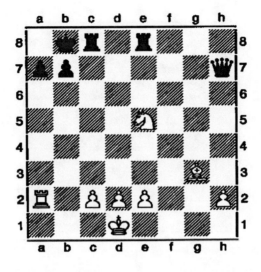

On the board above, it is white's turn to move. Do you see a force checkmate? **Nc6, Ka8**, then **Rxp** mate.

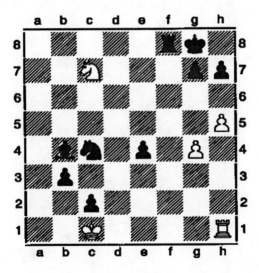

Look at the board above. Do you see the combination and checkmate for black? Look! Pawn moves to **e3**. The white rook will make an effort to stop the pawn from making a queen by moving to **h2**. Bishop would then move to **a3** with a checkmate!

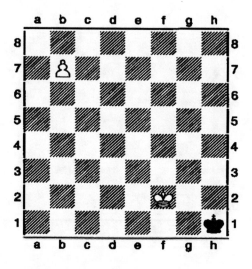

Look at the diagram above. White clearly has the advantage. White has to be careful. Checkmate can be accomplished in two moves or white can blunder and force a stalemate. Should white advance the pawn and ask for a queen? If this is done then that would be a stalemate. If white, however, advances the pawn to the eighth rank and asks for a rook, then the black king must move to **h2**. White would then move the rook to **h8** with a checkmate. Sometimes it is best not to ask for a queen when the pawn advances to the eighth rank.

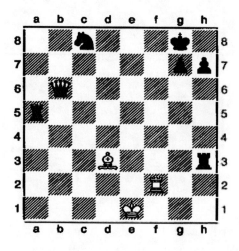

On the board above, black has a clear advantage, but it is white's turn to move. Do you see the combination for white? Okay Bishop moves to **c4** with a check. Black has two choices. One would give up the queen or the rook. Bishop will capture these pieces, and then the king will still have to move to **h8**. Rook will then move to **f8** with a checkmate.

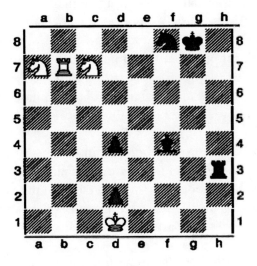

On the board above, it is black's turn to move. Do you see the checkmate? Answer: Black **d3** then **h1**

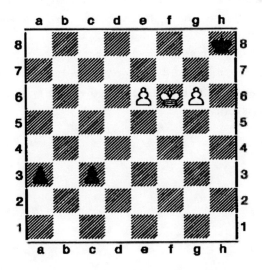

On the board above, it is white's turn to move. Do you see the combination? Okay. Pawn moves to **e7**. Either one of the pawns or the king will move. Pawn will then advance to **e8** for a queen. This is a checkmate!

Your End Game

Quite often, a player plays a beautiful opening and an excellent middle game, but fails to win because of a poor end game. Sometimes the winning move is within view, but for some reason, those moves are not seen. Your end game is a critical phase that complements both the opening and the middle games. Some players are very strong with their end games and are weak in their opening and middle games. All three phases of the game must be strengthened in order to achieve more wins.

It is also important to remember that in the opening and the middle game, the king is usually under attack from the major pieces and very often call on the pawns and other pieces for protection. In the end game, the king becomes an attacking piece and generally enters the game after all of the major pieces are off of the board. A king working with connected pawn in the end can be very effective.

Some players hate to record a draw. It is important to note that there is no dishonor if a draw is scored especially against a stronger player. Many end-game positions with pawns and the king usually end in draws. If a win cannot be achieved, then one should fight for a draw. A draw is not a loss.

The following are some end-game scenarios. Analyze each carefully and determine if:

A. White has a positional advantage and will win
B. Black has a positional advantage and will win
C. The game is a draw

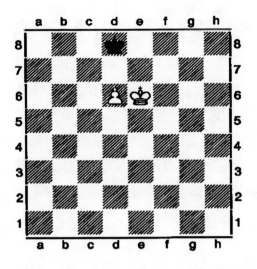

This was a well-played game, but a single move can determine if white will win, lose, or draw. Note that black cannot win this game. Black's only hope is to force a draw. It is white's turn to move. What is the best move for white?

Answer: The above game is actually a win for white if the correct move is executed. First, white must advance the pawn to **d7**. The black king cannot move to any other square but on **c7**. The white king will then move to **e7**. White will eventually advance the pawn to **d8** for a queen. A queen and the king give white major material advantage. White should win.

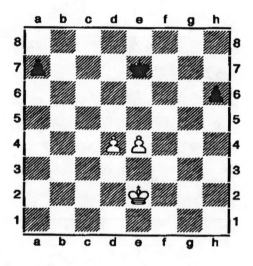

Look at the diagram above. It is black's turn to move. Is this a win or a loss for black or white? Is it a draw?

Answer: On the above board, it is very difficult for white to stop the two passed pawns. When the king attacks the pawn on the **h** *file,* the other pawn on the **a** *file* will advance. The two middle white pawns must be supported by the king in order to effectuate a win. It simply cannot support the middle pawns and still capture the two opposing black pawns. This is a win for black.

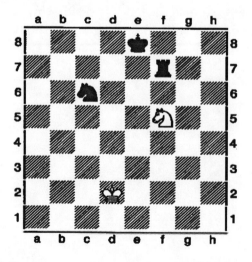

On the board above, it is white's turn to move. Is this a win, loss for black, or draw? Knight moves to **d6**. The rook is captured. A draw.

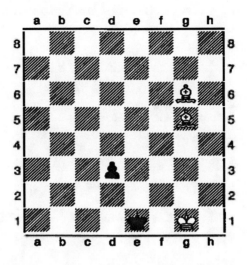

Examine this position very carefully. It is white's turn to move. Is this a win for white? A win for black? Or a draw?

Answer: This is a win for white. White must first move the bishop to **h5** to cut off the black diagonal line. Black then only has one move. Black must move the pawn to **c2**. White would then move the bishop to **h4** with a checkmate. This is beautiful!

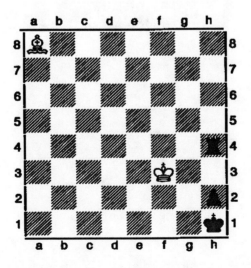

Here is another interesting position on the above board. Is this position a win for white? A win for black? Is it a draw? It is white's turn to move.

This is a win. King moves to **f2** with a check, rook moves to **e4**, bishop captures rook on **e4** with a checkmate!

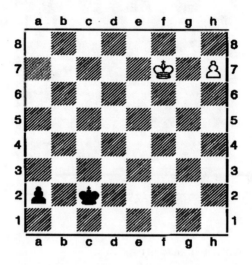

On the board above, it is white's turn to move. Is this a win or a draw? This a draw. The pawn advances to **h8** and obtain a queen. King would then move to **b1**, forcing a draw.

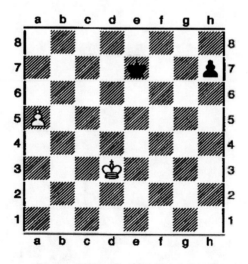

White is to move on the board above. Is this a win or a draw? This is a win for white. The king cannot stop the pawn on the file from reaching the eighth rank.

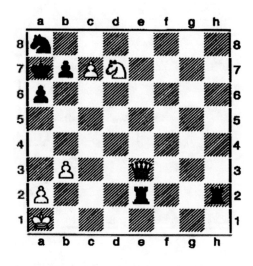

This is another beautiful game on the board above. It is white's turn to move. Who has the winning position? White or black? Is it a draw? Notice that black has material advantage and is getting ready to checkmate white on the **c1** square. What is the best move for white?

Answer: This is a win for white. White can advance the pawn to the eighth rank and obtain a queen, but black will use the opportunity to checkmate white. White has the advantage and should seize the opportunity. If the white pawn advances to the eighth rank and attains a *knight* instead of a queen, that would be *checkmate*.

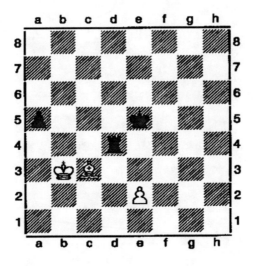

Look at the position on the board above. It is white's turn to move. What is the best move for white? Is it a win for white or black? Is it a draw?

Answer: This is another interesting position. Black is hoping that the bishop will capture the rook and force a draw. But wait! If the pawn moves to **e3,** white will win a free piece. Note that the white bishop has the black rook under a pin. The rook cannot move. White will eventually win this game.

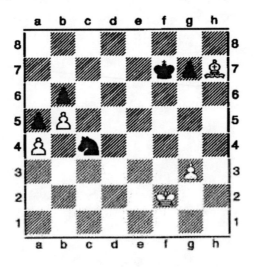

Look carefully at the position above. It is black's turn to move. What is the best move for black? It looks like a draw, isn't it? Is it a win for white or black?

Answer: This is not a draw. If black pawn moves to **g6**, the white bishop would be trapped. The king will eventually capture the bishop. Black would then have the advantage. This is a win for black.

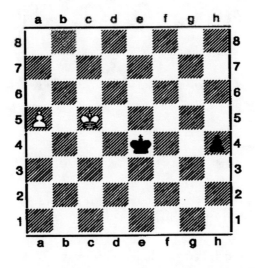

Look carefully at the board above. It is black's turn to move. Is it a win, a loss for black, or a draw?

Answer: This is a win for white. The black will promote and queen first, but when white pawn promotes to a queen, a check will be called. The black queen will be pinned and will be captured.

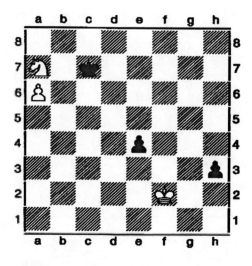

Examine the previous board carefully. It is black's turn to move. Is it a win for white or black? Is it a draw?

Answer: On the board, the two black pawns are working to reach to the first rank. One of the two pawns will advance to become a queen. The king cannot stop both. Black must sacrifice the pawn on **e4** by moving to **e3**. If the king eats, then the other pawn will advance to **h2** then **h1** for a queen. The king will not be able to stop this pawn. Black should win this game.

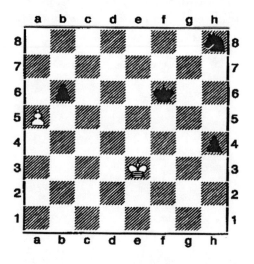

This is another interesting end game. It is white's turn to move. Is this a win for white or black? Is it a draw? What is the best move for white?

Answer: Examine the above game carefully. If the pawn on **a5** captures the pawn on **b6,** this could turn out to be a win for black. However, the pawn on a5 must advance to **a6** then to **a7** and then on **a8,** white would obtain a queen. This queen will stop black from obtaining a queen on **h1**. White will eventually win.

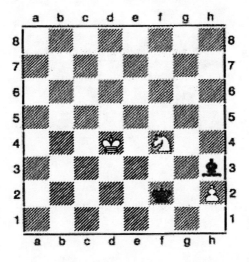

Look at where the white bishop and pawn are sitting. It is white's turn to move. Is this a win for white or black? Is this a draw? What is the best move for white?

Answer: This is a draw. Knight takes bishop with a check. King moves to g2. The knight or the pawn will eventually be capture.

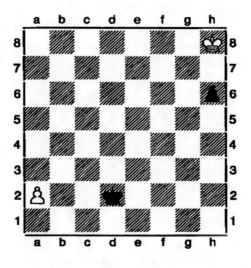

Look at the board above. White's to move. This is a win for white. The king cannot stop the pawn from reaching **a8**.

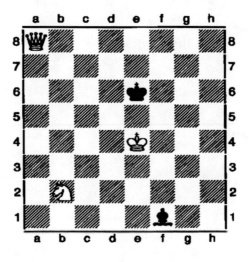

Look at the board above. It is black's turn to move. Is this a win, a loss for white, or a draw?

Answer: This is a draw. Bishop moves to **g2**. This move will capture the queen. The game cannot be won with just the bishop and the knight.

Chapter 14

Scenarios: Preparing for Checkmate

Each of the following scenarios can be solved in one or two moves. Find the checkmates in one or two moves.

Answers to these scenarios are listed on the last page.

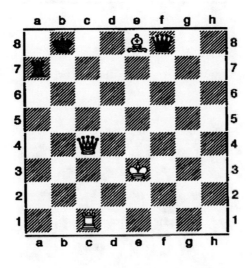

No. 1
White to move (mate in one)

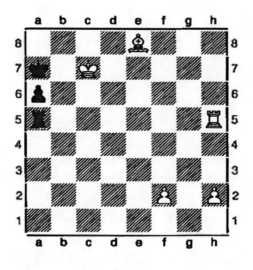

No. 2
White to move (mate in two)

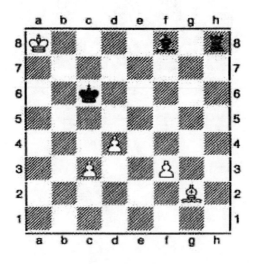

No. 3
Black to move (mate in one)

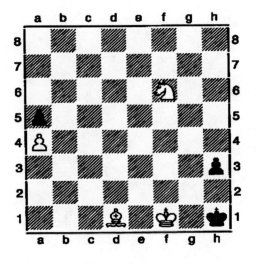

No. 4

White to move (mate in two)

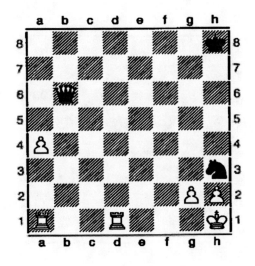

No. 5

Black to move (mate in two)

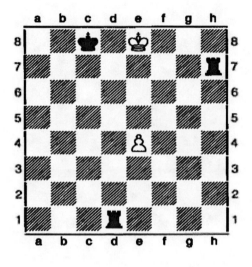

No.6

Black to move (mate in one)

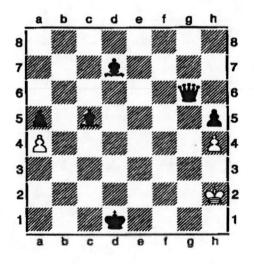

No. 7

Black to move (mate in one)

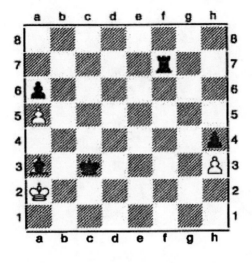

No. 8
Black to move (mate in two)

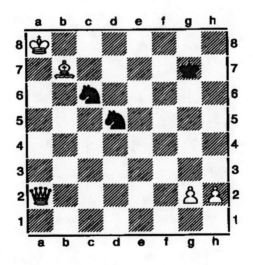

No.9
Black to move (mate in one)

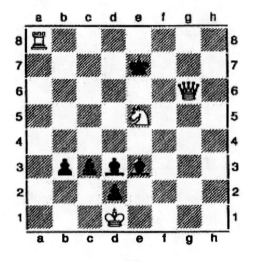

No. 10

Black to move (mate in one)

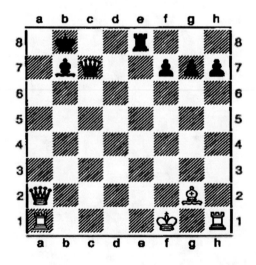

No. 11

White to move (mate in two)

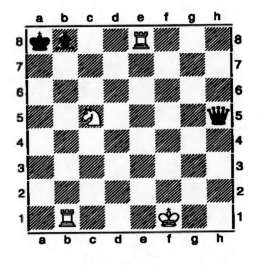

No. 12

White to move (mate in one)

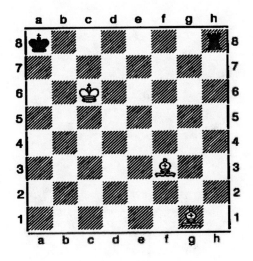

No. 13

White to move (mate in one)

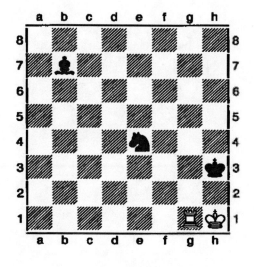

No. 14
Black to move (mate in one)

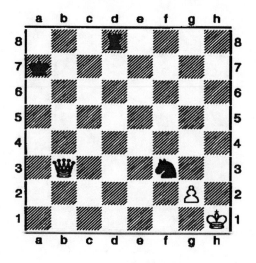

No. 15
Black to move (mate in one)

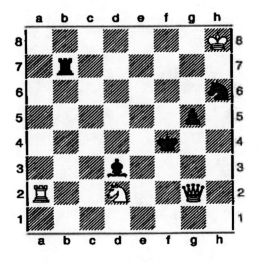

No. 16
Black to move (mate in one)

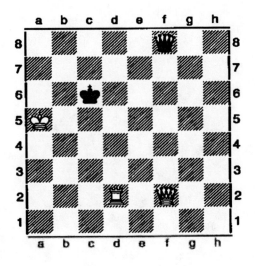

No. 17
Black to move (mate in one)

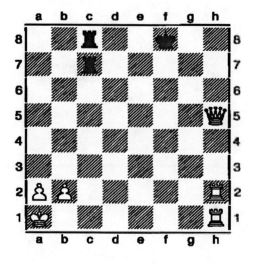

No. 18
Black to Move (mate in two)

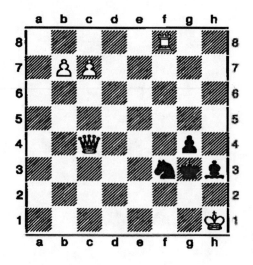

No.19
Black to move (mate in one)

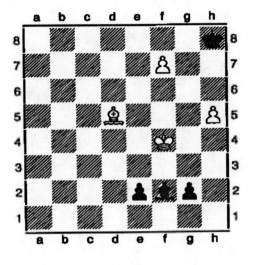

No. 20

White to move (mate in two)

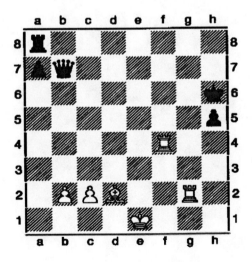

No. 21

White to move (mate in one)

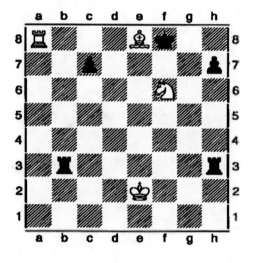

No. 22

Black to move (mate in two)

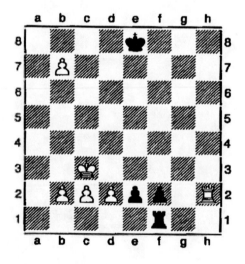

No. 23

White to move (mate in two)

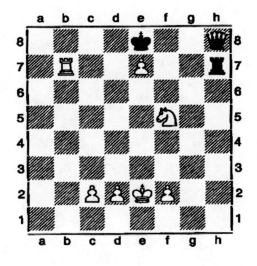

No. 24
White to move (mate in one)

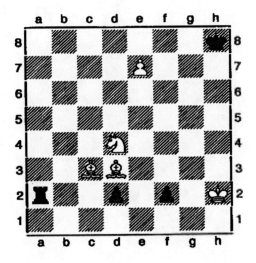

No. 25
White to move (mate in two)

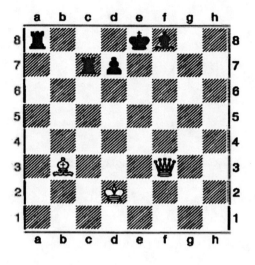

No. 26

White to move (mate in two)

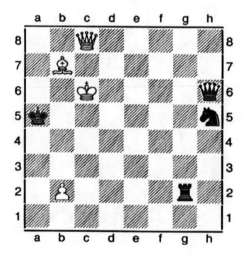

No. 27

White to move (mate in two)

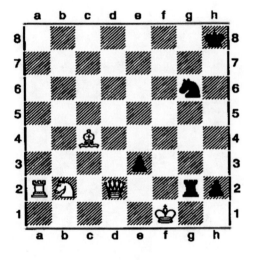

No. 28
Black to move (mate in one)

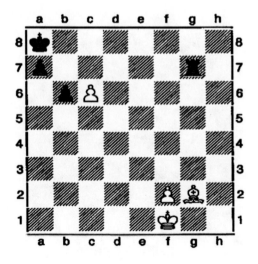

No. 29
White to move (mate in two)

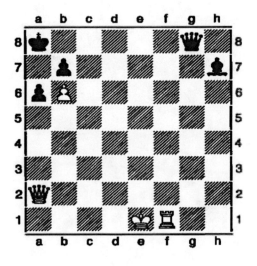

No. 30

White to move (mate in two)

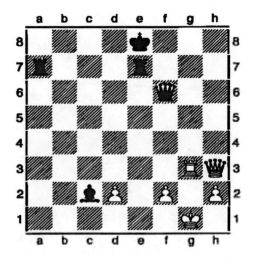

No. 31

White to move (mate in two)

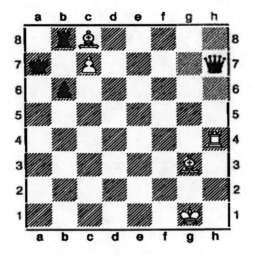

No. 32

White to move (mate in one)

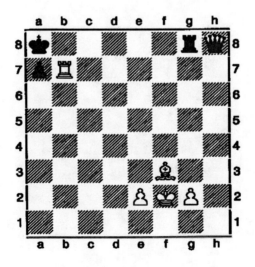

No. 33

White to move (mate in one)

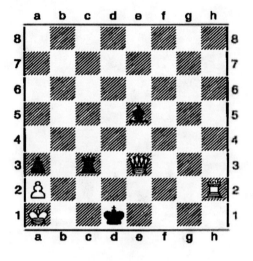

No. 34

Black to move (mate in one)

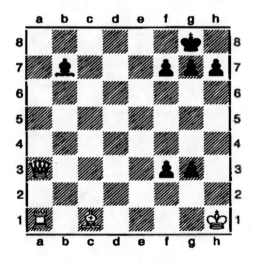

No. 35

Black to move (mate in two)

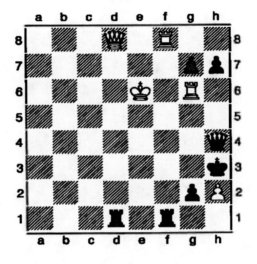

No. 36

Black to move (mate in one)

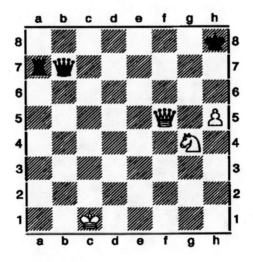

No. 37

White to move (mate in two)

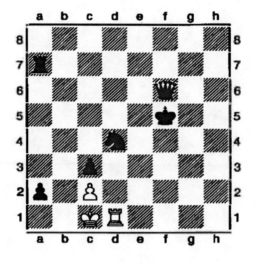

No. 38
Black to move (mate in one)

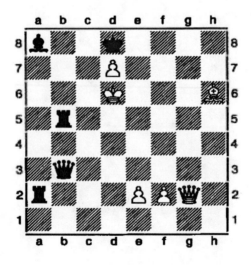

No. 39
White to move (mate in two)

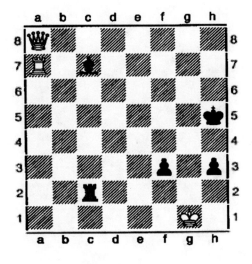

No. 40
Black to move (mate in two)

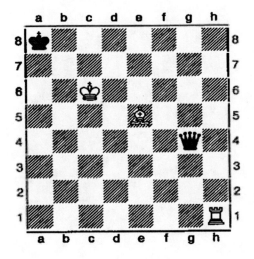

No. 41
White to move (mate in two)

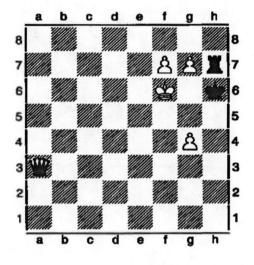

No. 42
White to move (mate in one)

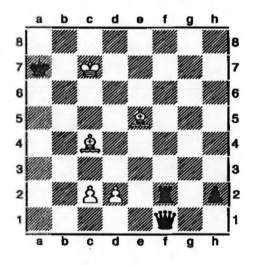

No. 43
White to move (mate in two)

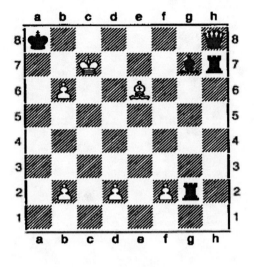

No. 44

White to move (mate in one)

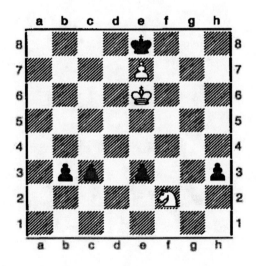

No. 45

White to move (mate in two)

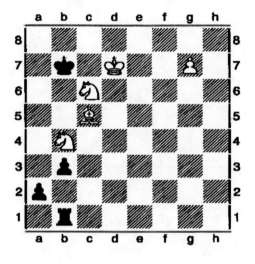

No. 46

White to move (mate in two)

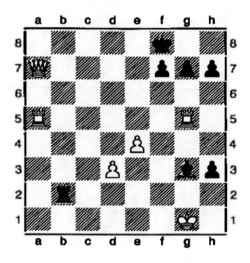

No. 47

Black to move (mate in one)

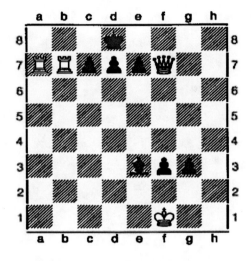

No. 48

Black to move (mate in two)

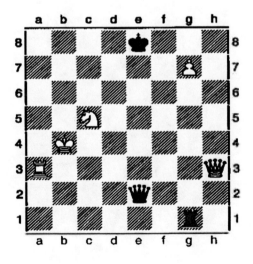

No. 49

White to move (mate in one)

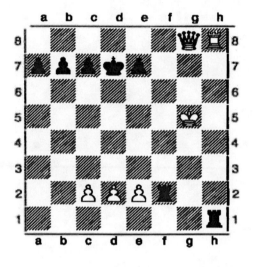

No. 50

Black to move (mate in two)

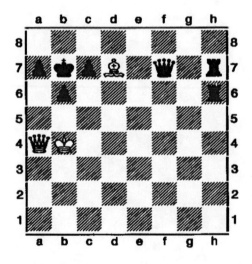

No. 51

White to move (mate in two)

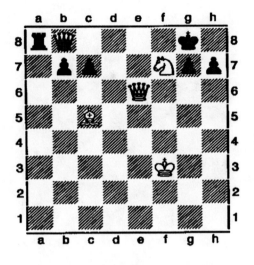

No. 52

White to move (mate in two)

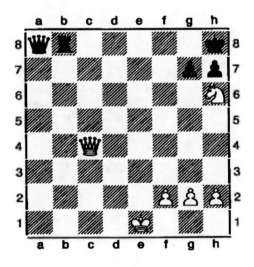

No. 53

White to move (mate in two)

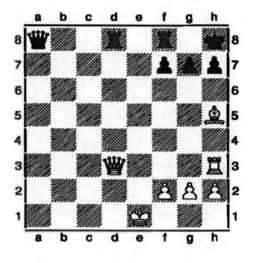

No. 54

White to move (mate in two)

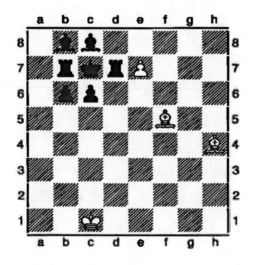

No. 55

White to move (mate in one)

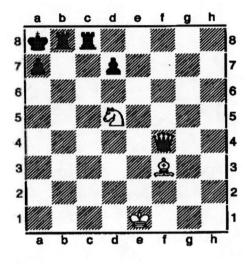

No. 56
White to move (mate in one)

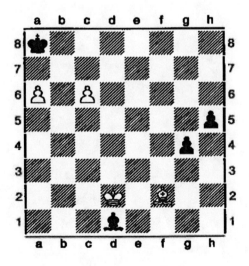

No. 57
White to move (mate in two)

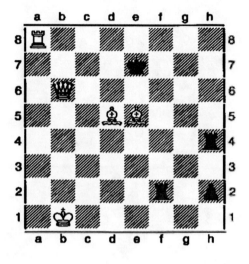

No. 58

Black to move (mate in two)

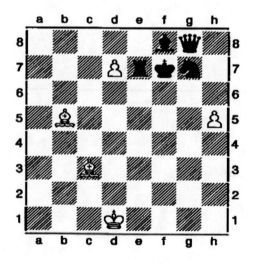

No. 59

White to move (mate in one)

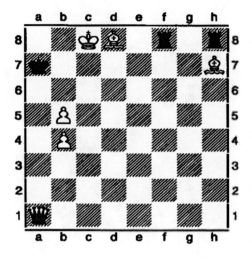

No. 60
White to move (mate in two)

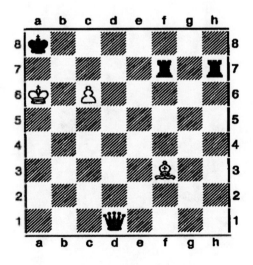

No. 61
White to move (mate in two)

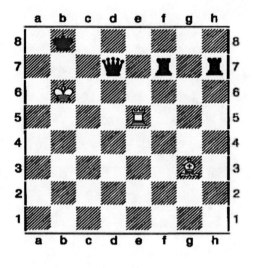

No. 62
White to move (mate in one)

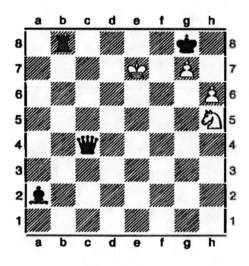

No. 63
White to Move. (mate in One)

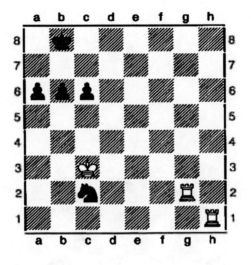

No. 64
White to move (mate in two)

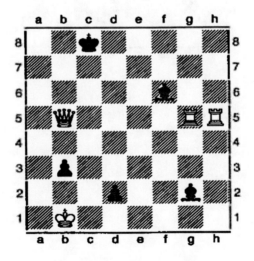

No. 65
Black to move (mate in one)

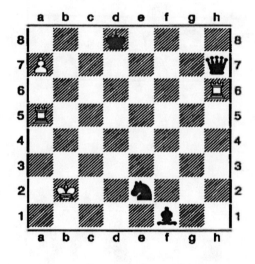

No. 66
White to move (mate in two)

The following scenarios are draws. Make the correct move.

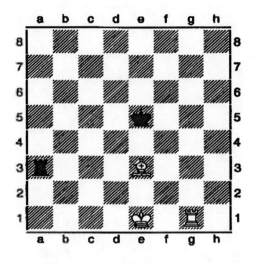

No. 67

Black to move (This is a forced draw.)

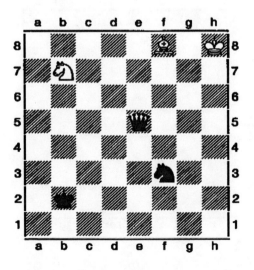

No. 68

White to move (This is forced draw.)

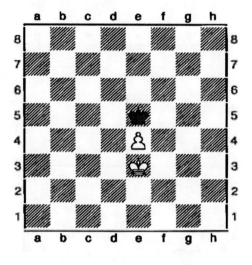

No. 69

Black to move (This is not a draw.)

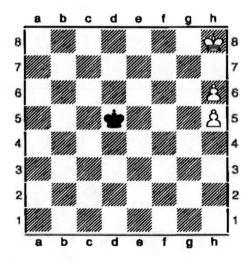

No. 70

Black to move (This is a draw.)

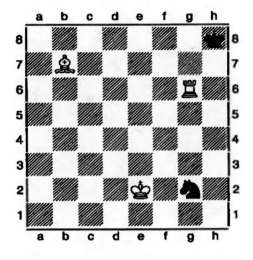

No. 71

Black to move (This is a draw.)

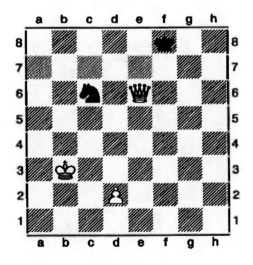

No. 72

Black to move. (This is a draw.)

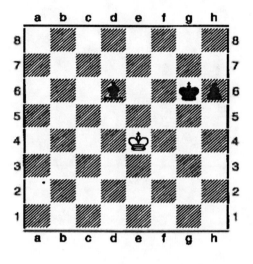

No. 73
Black to move (This is a draw.)

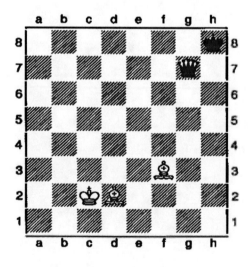

No. 74
White to move (A forced draw.)

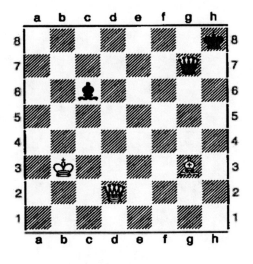

No. 75

White to move (A forced draw.)

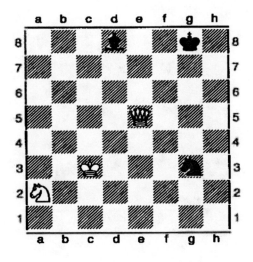

No. 76

Black to move (This is draw.)

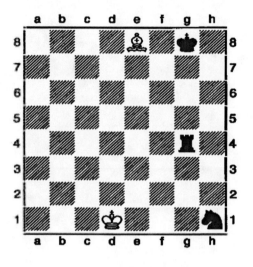

No.77
White to move (This is a draw.)

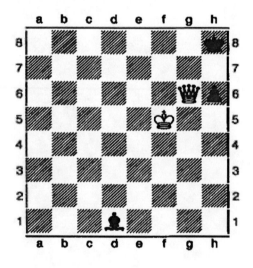

No.78
Black to move (This is a draw.)

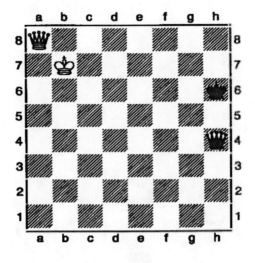

No.79

Black to move (This is a draw.)

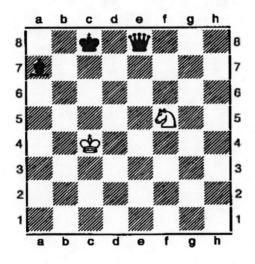

No. 80

White to move (This is a draw.)

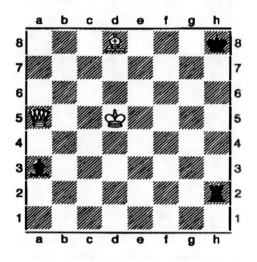

No. 81
Black to move (This is a draw.)

Winning Positional Advantages

Look at the following chessboard scenarios and tell whether white or black should win the game.

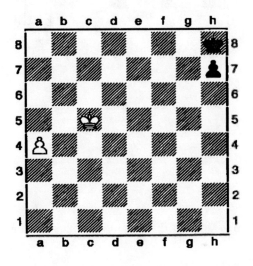

No. 82
Which side has the advantage? Black to move.

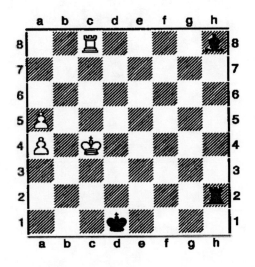

No. 83
Which side has the advantage? Black to move.

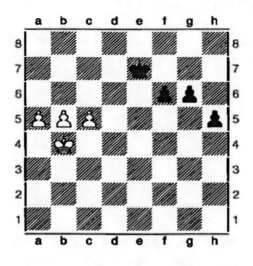

No. 84

Which side has the advantage? Black to move.

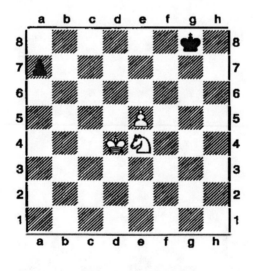

No. 85

Which side has the advantage? White to move.

Chapter 15

Important Chess Terms

All chess players should be armed with a basic chess vocabulary. The following terms are often used in chess. All prospective chess players should become familiar with these chess words. A player's game can effectively improve when the element of the game of chess is practiced and executed.

Chess Terms and Meanings

1. Adjust
    -   A word that is used to indicate that a player is intentionally touching a piece to place it legally in the center of a given square.

2. Advantage
    -   When the chess pieces are placed in a position to win.
    -   Superior development.
    -   Superior structure of pieces and pawns.

3. Attack
    -   To execute a series of moves against an opponent with the hope of capturing pawns or pieces or gaining superior position.

4. Back-rank
    -   The eighth or first rank that is occupied by any of the enemy pieces.
    -   Another name for the first rank. The rank behind the pawns in the starting position.

5. Backward pawn
    -   A pawn that cannot be supported by other adjoining pawns. The supportive pawns are too far advanced to protect the weaker pawn.

6. Blocked

- A defensive strategy that is used to prevent one pawn or some pieces from advancing or moving forward.

7. Blunder

- A mistake that turns the balance of the game into a winning position or a positional advantage for the opposing player.

8. Castling

- A special move in chess involving the king and the rook of the same color moving at the same time. This move is designed to protect the king, and it is considered to be one move.

9. Check

- A word that is used to indicate that the king is under a direct attack.

10. Checkmate

- The ultimate aim of the chess player. The trapping of the king and gaining a winning position.
- Placing the king in an inescapable position.
- The forced ending to a chess game.

11. Combination

- A series of moves to benefit the initiator or the person who is executing those moves.

12. Connected pawns

- Pawns that move in unison with other pawns along the same rank, file, or diagonally. These pawns protect each other while advancing.

13. Control

- Dominance of a particular position, the stage of the game or square on the check board.

14. Decoy
- A tactical idea in which an enemy piece is forced to move or capture on a particular square.

15. Defense
- A single or a series of moves that are designed to counteract an opponent attack.

16. Development
- Bringing one piece or pieces into play. The effectiveness of this move starts at the beginning of a game.

17. Discovered attack
- A tactical move that is used by moving a piece, and in so doing, opens a line of attack against a separate piece.

18. Double check
- Moving a piece and putting the enemy king in check twice.

19. Double pawns
- Two or more pawns of the same color on the same file.

20. Draw
- A game that does not end in a decisive victory for any player. Each player receives one-half point.

21. En passant
- When the capture of a pawn is made by not occupying the same square of the piece being captured.

22. Exchange
- To capture an opponent piece with the understanding that the opponent will recapture.
- To trade or swap

23. Fianchetto
- A flanked development of a bishop by placing it on the **b2**, **h2**, **b7**, or **h7** files.

24. File
- One of the columns that runs vertically on the chessboard.

25. Forced
- A move or series of moves for which there is no alternative for one or both players.

26. Fork
- A tactical move in which one attacks two pieces at the same time.

27. Gambit
- An opening sacrifice of a pawn to gain an attack and the initiative.

28. Hanging piece
- An unprotected piece or a pawn that is exposed to be captured.

29. Initiative
- To gain the advantage in order to control the flow of a game.
- To create a threat.

30. Interpose
- To block an attack by placing a piece between the enemy piece and the piece that is under attack.

31. Isolated pawn
- A pawn that is not supported by another pawn or another piece.

32. Major piece
- A queen and a rook are major pieces.

33. Mate
- A shorter word for checkmate

34. Material
- More quality pieces or pawns that are controlled by one person.

- More valuable pieces.

35. Middle game
- The second phase of the game that comes after the opening moves and before the end game.

36. Minor Pieces
- The bishop and the knight are considered as minor pieces.

37. Open Files
- A file where there is no pawns or other pieces on it.

38. Opening
- The first stage of a chess game. This is when both players fight for the control of the center of the board and to gain slight or major advantages.

39. Opposition
- A standoff between two kings

40. Overworked
- When a piece has too many jobs to perform.

41. Passed Pawn
- A pawn that has no enemy pawns blocking its path.

42. Pieces
- Some of the thirty-two units on the chessboard to include the knights, bishops, rooks, queens, or kings. Pawns are referred to as pawns.

43. Pin
- A tactical move that is used to prevent an enemy piece from moving off of a particular square for fear of exposing another important piece to an attack.

44. Passive move
- Holding back. Not becoming aggressive.

45. Perpetual Check
- Never ending or repeating continuously. No end in sight.

46. Promotion
-    The changing of a pawn for a major or a minor piece.

47. Rank
-    The numbered horizontal rows on the chess board.

48. Rating
-    A numbered system that is employed for different chess federations to score the strength of a player as compared to other players.

49. Resign
-    To end a chess game with a verbal acknowledgement that the game is lost.

50. Skewer
-    A tactical move by which an attack is made along a line that contains two valuable pieces one behind the other. Usually the piece that is behind is the most valuable piece.

51. Sufficient Material
-    Enough mating pieces. Insufficient material is not having enough mating pieces.

52. Tempo
-    A useful move that aids in gaining an advantage.

53. Time Pressure
-    The shortage of time on one's clock, forcing that player to hurry the moves.

54. Touch move
-    If a player touches a piece. It must be moved.

55. Touch take
-    If a player touches an opponent piece with the intention of taking it, that piece must be taken.

56. Trade

- An even exchange of pieces

57. Trap

- Forcing or luring an opponent to capture a piece which would lead to the loss of pieces or the game.

58. Variation

- A series of moves in which an opponent makes a series of moves sometimes outside the line of the main structured moves.

59. Weak pawn

- A pawn which is not protected and can easily be attacked or taken by an opponent pie.

60. Weakness

- An area on the board that can easily be attacked or taken advantage of by an opponent.

Chapter 16

World Chess Champions

To become a champion in any sport, one has to listen, work hard, build on the experience of others, be disciplined, and devote time and energy. Champions believe in themselves. The following persons who reigned as world champions did not experience success overnight. They toiled, listened to others, started at an early age, and built on little achievements one game at a time.

Basic Facts about Past and Present World Chess Champions from 1886 to the Present

William Steinitz
- Reigned officially as the First World Chess Champion from 1886 to 1894.
- Born 1836 and died 1900
- First official World Chess Champion.
- Five feet tall
- Born in Austrian Empire, in the city of Prague.
- An Austrian, English, American chess player.
- He and Paul Murphy are said to be the founder of modern chess.
- Learned to play chess at the age of twelve
- Began to play chess as a professional at the age of twenty-six.
- When he became a citizen of the United States, he changed his first name to William.
- He was the last of thirteen children.
- A talented mathematician and a top scholar.

- Undefeated in chess competition in thirty years.
- He was a Jew
- He died as a pauper.

Emanuel Lasker
- Reigned as the second World Chess Champion from 1894 to 1921
- Born 1868 and died 1942
- Second official World Chess Champion
- Born in Germany
- Defeated William Steinitz
- Maintained the world championship title for twenty-seven years.
- Distinguished mathematician and philosopher
- Friend of Albert Einstein
- Learned to play chess at the age of eleven.
- At the age of twenty-one, he won the title in Germany as the Master of Chess.
- World champion at the age of twenty-five. Lost to Capablanca

Jose Raul Capablanca
- Reigned as the third World Chess World Champion from 1921 to 1927
- The third official World Chess Champion
- Born 1888 and died 1942
- Born in Cuba
- Learned the rules of chess at the age of four.
- At the age of thirteen, he defeated the Cuban National Champion
- He defeated the US champion when he was twenty-nine years old.
- Undefeated as a world champion for eight years. He won sixty-three straight competitive tournament games.
- He refused to read a chess book or study openings.
- Greatest natural chess player
- Died at the age of fifty-two while reviewing a game, at the Manhattan Chess Club.

Alexander Alekhine
- Reigned as the fourth World Chess Champion from 1927 to1935
- Born into a wealthy Russian family in Russia.
- His mother taught him chess when he was a young boy.

- Became a naturalized French citizen and a French grandmaster
- Participated in his first known chess tournament at the age of ten—He defeated Capablanca to attain the fourth World Champion.
- He played tournament games against Capablanca before the World Chess Championship tournament, and he was never once defeated Capablanca.
- After he won the World Champion, he lost only seven games out of 238 tournament matches from 1927 to 1935.
- He lost his first title to Max Euwe, the Dutch grandmaster. It is widely believed that alcohol affected Alekhine in this tournament.
- He gave up alcohol and regained his championship from Max Euwe in 1937.
- After Max Euwe, he won the World Chess Championship and became the sixth World Chess Champion after max Euwe.
- He was the fourth and the sixth World Chess Champion.

Machgielis Euwe
- Reigned as the fifth World Chess Champion from 1935 to 1936
- He was the fifth World Chess Champion.
- Born in 1901 and died 1983
- His mother taught him chess at the age of four.
- Born in Holland. He was a Dutch grandmaster
- Became Dutch National Champion from 1921 to 1958
- A doctorate degree in mathematics
- Defeated Alekhine to gain the championship
- After he became champion, he won a total of 102 tournament games.
- 1970 FIDE president

Alexander Alekhine
- Reigned again as the World Chess Champion
- He reigned from 1937 to 1946
- During this period, he represented the country of France.

Mikhail Botvinnik
- Reigned as the seventh World Chess Champion from 1948 to 1957 and from 1958 to 1960 and also from 1961 to 1963.
- Born in part of Finland that is now part of Russia
- Born in 1911 and died in 1995
- A Russian Jew

- He was first noticed in the eyes of the world when he defeated Capablanca in an exhibition game, at the age of fourteen.
- He learned the game at the age of twelve.
- At age twenty, he won the first major chess tournament in Russia.
- He had a degree in electrical engineering.

Vasily Smyslov
- Reigned as the World Chess Champion from 1957 to 58
- Born in Russia in 1921, he is now eighty-six years old.
- His father taught him how to play chess at an early age.
- At age seventeen, he won the Russia Junior Chess Champion
- He was twice the Soviet Union Chess Champion from 1949 to 55.
- Won seventeen Chess Olympiad medals, an all-time record.
- Became a Soviet Union National Chess Master in his late teens.
- Known for his positional style and precise handling of end games.
- Contributed to the theory in many chess openings such as the English opening and the Sicilian Defence

Mikhail Botvinnik
- Became the World Champion again on 1958-1960

Mikhail Tal
- Reigned as World Chess Champion from 1960 to1961
- Born in Riga, Latvia, Russia, in 1936 and died in 1992
- He defeated Mikhail Botvinnik when he was twenty-three years old. At that time, he was the youngest grandmaster to become a World Chess Champion.
- He learned to play chess when he was eight years old.
- He began to study chess seriously when he became a teenager.
- Defeated Mikhail Botvinnik in 1960 when he was twenty-three years old. Botvinnik was then the world chess champion.
- He suffered ill health most of his life.
- He was known as an attacking genius who had the ability to analyze and solve complex problems.
- Had a degree in literature.
- He was a schoolteacher for twenty years.
- Became the USSR chess champion when he was twenty years old.
- Became the sixth- time Soviet Union Chess champion.
- A member of the Russian Olympic team that won eight goal medals.

Mikhail Botvinnik 1961-1963
- Reigned again as World Champion after defeating Mikhail Tal

Tigran Petrosian
- Reigned as World Champion from 1963 to 1969
- Born in 1929 and died in 1984
- Nicknamed Iron Tigran due to his playing style and defense
- Candidate for the World Champion on ten different occasions
- He was the Soviet Union champion four different times.
- He learned to play chess at the age of eight.
- Defeated Mikhail Botvinnik in 1963.
- He believes in the building up of small advantages.
- A Soviet and international chess grandmaster
- Prior to studying chess full time, he was a caretaker and a road sweeper.
- Defended his title in 1963, defeating Boris Spassky. Petrosian became the first champion to win a match as champion.
- The only player to break Bobby Fischer's winning streak of twenty games in 1971.
- Two different major openings are named after him. The Petrogian Variations.

Boris Spassky
- Reigned as the tenth World Chess Champion from 1969 to 1972.
- Born in 1937 in Russia.
- He represented both Russia and France in World Champion matches.
- He was the Soviet Union chess champion twice from 1961 to 1973
- World candidate on seven occasions.
- One of the world's top ten players from 1950 to the mid-1980s.
- Learned to play chess on a train at the age of five.
- In 1947, at the age of ten, he defeated the Soviet Union chess champion Botvinnik in an exhibition game.
- He became the youngest Soviet player to make rank of candidate for grandmaster at the age of eleven, and grandmaster at the age of fifteen.
- At age eighteen, he became a FIDE International Grandmaster.
- Beat Petrosian to attain the World Champion in 1969.
- Lost to Bobby Fischer in 1972.

- He was embarrassed when he lost to Fischer. He felt that he has let down a whole nation especially during the height of the cold war.
- He migrated to France and played for the French Olympic team
- He became a French citizen in 1978.

Robert J. Fischer 1972-1975
- Born on March 9, 1943, in Chicago, USA.
- He was the only US-born official World Chess Champion.
- He became the Chess World Champion in 1972.
- Some argued that he was the greatest chess player of all time.
- He was living in Iceland and died in January, 2008, at the age of 64.
- Learned how to play chess by reading the instruction on a chess set that was owned by his sister. This occurred when he was only six years old.
- He learned to play chess on his own for over a year, then he joined a few active chess clubs. Later, his mother provided him with a personal tutor.
- He dropped out of high school. Some of his teachers said that he was a difficult student with an incredible retention memory.
- Won the US Junior Chess Champion in 1956.
- At the age of twelve, he was awarded the title of US National Chess Master.
- In 1957, at the age of fourteen, he won the US Open Chess Champion. He became the youngest chess champion.
- At the age of fifteen, he competed in a number of international chess tournaments. He played against some of the world top players and was very successful in most of the matches. Many of the world masters were rather surprised of his ability.
- In 1961, in Bled, he met Tal for the first time and defeated him. Fischer was the only player from this world tournament who went undefeated.
- He had a disappointing showing in the next world tournament that was held in Curacao.
- At age nineteen, he was referred to as the world's strongest player who is a non Soviet.
- He won all of the US Championship Tournament between 1952-1964
- He was forced to return to school in 1958 to complete his high school education.

- Played firts board for the US in four World Olympic Tournaments
- He defeated the Russian-born Boris Spassky in 1972, at the height of the cold war, and became the World Chess Champion.

Anatoly Karpov

- Reigned as the Chess World Champion from 1975 to 1985.
- Born in Russia on May 23, 1951.
- Some people consider him as the most successful tournament player at all times.
- As of July 2005, he had won 161 first-place finishes in tournament games.
- From 1978 to 1998, he played in every FIDE World Champion match.
- His overall record in world tournament matches 1,118 wins, 278 Losses, and 1,480 draws, in 3,163 games.
- He became a candidate for chess master at the age of eleven.
- He became the youngest Soviet Union National Chess Master at the age of fifteen in 1966.
- In his first international chess tournament, he placed first.
- He was an academically gifted student.
- Karpov never played Bobby Fischer.
- Fischer drew up a list of demand when he was about to play Karpov for the championship title. FIDE, the governing body then, refused to accept Fischer's demands.
- Fischer refused to play Karpov under FIDE rules and resigned as the World Champion.
- Karpov automatically became the world champion when Fischer resigned.
- Karpov represented the Soviet Union in six World Olympic Chess tournaments and help his team six won gold for the Soviet.
- Kasparov defeated Karpov in one of the most difficult and hardest—fought matches ever.
- Karpov's rating once reached 2,985, the highest performance rating for any chess player in tournament history. Bobby Fischer's highest rating was 2881.

Garry Kasparov 1985-2000

- Born in Russia, on April 13, 1963 as Garri Veinstein
- His mother was an American. His father died when he was seven years old. He then adopted his mother's surname, Kasparyan, which later changed to the Russian version as Kasparov.

- Kasparov became the youngest ever World Chess Champion in 1985.
- He learned to play chess before he was seven years old. At age ten, he attended a prestigious chess school in Russia.
- He won the Soviet Junior Chess Championship in 1978 when he was fifteen years old. He also became a chess master and became the youngest player to qualify for the Soviet Championship when he was fifteen years old.
- He reigned as the World Chess Champion for fifteen years.-He was defeated by Valdimir Kramnik in 2000.
- Became the first player to lose in a World Championship match without winning a game since 1921.
- Retired from serious chess competition in 2005.
- Kasparov holds the record for the player to hold the longest time the number 1 rated player in the world.
- Kasparov's highest rating reached to 2,851
- In 1989, Kasparov defeated a computer Deep Thought in a two- game match.
- In 1996, he played against an IBM computer, Deep Blue. Kasparov lost the first game but eventually won the match.
- In 1997, he played against an updated version of Deep Blue and narrowly lost.
- In 2002, he played against Deep Junior. This match ended in a draw.
- In 2003, he drew a match against X3D Fritz, another computer.
- Today, Kasparov is actively involved in politics in Russia.

Vladimir Kramnik 2000-2006
- Born on June 25, 1975, in Russia
- World Chess Champion from 2000 to 2007
- He learned chess while he was child and later studied this sport in school while in elementary school.
- He beat Kasparov in a sixteen-game match and became the Classical World Chess Champion.
- He successfully defended his title in 2004.
- Kramnik became the first undisputed World Champion holding both the FIDE and the Classical title since Kasparov in 1993.
- He won a gold metal in 1992 for the Soviet team in the Chess Olympiad tournament in Manila. He was only sixteen years at that time and had received the ranking of master at that time.
- In 2002, he competed and draw against the computer Deep Fritz.

- In 2006, he had a rematch against Deep Fritz and lost.
- He lost his title to Viswanathan Anand, from India, in September 2007.

Viswanathan Anand
- Born on December 11, 1969 in the country of India.
- Anand became the fourth player on the FIDE rating list to reach beyond 2,800 rating points.
- In April, 2007, Anand was ranked first in the world.
- In September 2007, he became the undisputed World Chess Champion.
- Anand became the youngest Indian to win the World Junior Chess Champion in 1988.
- At the age of eighteen, he became the first Indian grandmaster.
- Anand worn the Chess Oscar in 1997, 1998, 2003, and 2004. He became the third non-Russian player to so. The other players were Bobby Fischer of the United States and Bent Larsen of Denmark.

The Chess Oscar is awarded to the world's best chess player for a particular. This decisions is made by journalists, world polls, and chess critics.
- Anand became the National Chess Champion of India when he was sixteen years old.
- He became the FIDE world champion in 2000, becoming the first Indian to win that title.
- He lost title in 2002 to a Russian, but he won back the title in September 2007 against another Russian. He is scheduled to defend his title in 2008.
- In 2003, FIDE organized a World Rapid Chess tournament with some of the best rapid players in the world. Anand won this tournament without losing one game.

Answers to Scenarios

1. Q-c8 #
2. 1.RxR 1.K-a8
   2. RxP#
3. B-c5#
4. 1. B-F3 1.K-h2
   2. N-g4#
5. 1. Q-g1 1. RxQ

2. N-f2#
6. R-d8#
7. Q-g1#
8. 1. R-f1 1.Kxb
    2. R-a1#
9. N-c7#
10. c2#
11. 1. Q-a8 1.BXQ
    2. RXB#
12. R-a1#
13. K-c7#
14. N-f2#
15. R-h8#
16. R-h7#
17. Q-a3#
18. 1.R-c1 1. RXR 2. RXR#
19. B-g2#
20. 1. f8/Q 1. K-h7
    2. B-e4#
21. R-f7#
22. 1. R-b2 1. K-d1
    2. R-h1#
23. 1. R-h7 1. K-f8 or d8
    2. b8/Q #
24. N-d6#
25. 1. N-e6 1. K-g8
    2. e8/Q#
26. 1. Q-f7 1. K-d8
    2. QXB#
27. 1. Q-f5 1. K-a4 or b4
    2. Q-b5#
28. h1/Q#
29. 1. c7 1.RXB
    2. c8#
30. 1. QXQ 1. BXQ
    2. R-f8#
31. 1. Q-c8 1. K-f7
    2. Q-g8#
32. R-a4#

33. R-b6#
34. R-c1#
35. f2#
36. Q-e1#
37. 1. Q-f8 1. K-h7
    2. N-f6#
38. N-e2#
39. 1. B-g5 1. RXB
    2. QXR#
40. 1. h2 1. K-f1 2.h1/Q# or
    2. h2 1.K-h1 2.R-c1#
41. 1.R-a1#
42. g8/N#
43. 1. B-d4 1.K-a8
    2. B-d5#
44. B-d5#
45. 1. N-g4 1.h2
    2. Nf6#
46. 1. N-a5 1. K-a8
    2. a8/Q#
47. R-b1#
48. 1. g2 1.K-e1
    2. g1/Q#
49. Q-d7#
50. 1.R-g1 1. K-H5
    2. R-h2#
51. 1. Q-a6 1. KxQ
    2. B-c8 or 1.Q-a6 2. K-a8 2.Q-c8#
52. 1.N-d8 1.K-h8
    2. Q-e8#
53. 1.Q-g8 1RXg8
    2. N-f7#
54. 1. Qxh7 1. KxQ
    2. Bxf7 mate
55. 1. e8/Knight mate
56. 1. Nc7 mate
57. 1. c7 1. Pawn or Bishop move
    2. c8/Q mate
58. Black White

h1 Bxp

Rxb mate

59. d8/Knight-mate
60. 1. b6 1. K-a6 or a8

    2. Bd3 or e4-mate
61. White C7 check, then QXB, pawn promote to e8 for a queen. Checkmate.
62. Rook to e8 checkmate
63. Knight to f6—checkmate
64. Rook to h8 then Rg7.
65. Be4
66. Pawn promotes to a8 for a queen. King to the seventh rank. Ra7-checkmate.
67. RxB Rook vs. a Rook should be a draw.
68. White—Bg7 pinning the queen Queen takes bishop. King takes bishop
69. King moves to f3 black king moves to e6 When King moves to f4, King must move on f6 the same side. Continue this pattern. When the white king reaches on the e7 rank, the black king should be standing on the e8 square.
70. Black—King must get to the h1 square
71. Black—Kf4 forking the rook
72. Black—Nd4 forking the queen
73. White—King move to h1. The black bishop is unable to help.
74. White—Bc3 forking the queen.
75. White—Qc3 forcing the exchange
76. Black—bf6 pinning the queen, QxB, then N forks Queen.
77. White-Bh5 with a pin.
78. Black-Bc2 pinning the queen.
79. Black-Qe4 pinning the queen. QxQ
80. White-Nd6 folking the queen.
81. Black—Rh5 pinning the queen.
82. White has the advantage. White should win.
83. Black Rc2 check and win the rook. Black has the advantage.
84. White has the advantage. Pawn will reach to a8 first. (a promotion to a queen)
85. White has the advantage.

Bibliography

Bardwick, Todd, *Chess Workbook for Children the Chess Detective's Introduction to the Royal Game*, Chess Detective Press, Eaglewood, Colorado, 2006.

Chernev, Irving and Fred Reinfield. *Winning Chess*, Simon and Schuster, New York, 1975.

Lasker, Emmanuel. *Lasker's Manual of Chess*, Dover Publishing, Inc. New York, 1947.

MacEnulty, David. *The Chess Kid's Book of Tactics*, Random House Puzzles and Games, New York, 2003.

Wilson, Fred and Bruce Alberston. *202 Checkmates for Children*, Cardoza Publishing, New York, 2004.

FIDE Handbook: Chess Rules (http://www.fide.com/official/handbook. asp?level=EE10, adopted at the 75 Fide Congress at Calvia, Mallorca, 2004

Wikipedia contributors, "World Chess Championship" Wikipedia, the free encyclopedia (http://en.wikipedia.org/wiki/World_Chess_ Championship, undated, accessed, September 12, 2007

Wikipedia contributors, "Chess Tactics" Wikipedia, the free encyclopedia (http://en.wikipedia.org/wilki/Chess_tactics, modified, August 2007.

Wikipedia contributors, "Sicilian Defence," Wikipedia, the Free Encyclopedia.http://en.wikipedia.org/wiki/Sicilian_Defence. Accessed March 4, 2008.

Wikipedia contributors, "King Gambit," Wikipedia, the Free Encyclopedia. http://en.wikipedia.org/wiki/King's_Gambit. Accessed September 5, 2007.

The history of the chess pieces (http://library.think quest.org/C001348/ international/pieces/his_pieces_en.html. Accessed July, 2007.

Wheeler, David A. The Beginner's Garden of Chess Openings (http://www. dwheeler.com/chess-openings/ Accessed, September, 2007.

Additional Credit

Chessbase Gmbh, 22297 Hamburg, Germany
e-mail: info@chessbase.com
internet: www.chessbase.de
For the use of the chessbase CD.

Index

A

accumulation of queens. *See* pawns:
    promotion to queens
algebraic notation, 94
Anderssen, Adolf, 25

B

bishop, 23, 47
  capture, 52
  movements, 47, 49
  value, 48
  white bishops, 48
bishop (history)
  representation of the church, 47
  sailing ships, 47

C

Capablanca, Jose. *See* Capablanca,
    Jose Raul under World Chess
    Champion
Caro, Horation, 114
castling, 53, 71
  illegal move, 73, 76
  legal move, 73
  movements, 73
championship games, 25
check, 100
checkmate, 30, 53, 55, 63, 65, 83, 100,
    182
chess, 15, 19, 26, 92
  basic chess information, 15
  basic principles, 15
  chess teachers, 15

etiquette of the game, 15, 100, 174
players, 15, 19, 20, 54, 86
social and intellectual benefits, 26
students, 15
 gameoflife, 15
chessboard, 15, 20, 21, 25, 31, 39, 42,
    47, 49, 60, 63, 68, 71, 167
diagonal squares, 21
files (vertical squares), 19, 21
ranks (horizontal squares), 19, 21
chess clock, 168
chess clubs, 25
chess game, 15
  center games, 167
  corner the king, 68
  democratic process to begin a game,
    86
  end games, 167
  history of pieces, 15
  movement of pieces, 15
  openings, 167
  position the board, 15
  simple method in choosing colors,
    86
  tournament, 86
  tournament arbitrator, 25, 86, 169
chess origin
  Arabs, 61
  India or Afghanistan, 25
  Spaniards, 61
chess pieces
  black, 20, 21
  thirty-two, 20
  white, 20, 21
chess promotion
  chess federations, 26

community tournament, 26
different schools, 26
neighborhood clubs, 26
online sites, 26
chess symbols, 92
chess tactics
    braking the pin, 132
    decoy, 121, 137
    deflection, 121, 145
    discovered check, 121, 135
    double check, 121, 152
    forcing a daw, 121, 162
    fork, 121
    fork:bishop fork, 123
    fork:knight fork, 125
    fork:pawn fork, 122
    fork:queen fork, 126
    offering a daw, 160
    overload, 121, 141
    pin, 121, 128
    pin:absolute pin, 128
    pin:relative pin, 128
    removing the guard, 121, 158
    skewer, 121, 155
chess tournaments
    held in many countries, 26
    through computer, 26

D

draw. *See* stalemate

E

en passant. *See* pawn movements

F

Fédéracion Internationale des Échecs,
    27, 109
FIDE. *See* Fédéracion Internationale
    des Échecs
fifty-move rule, 108
first international chess tournament
    (London), 25

Fischer, Bobby. *See* Fischer, Robert J.
    under World Chess Champion
forms of notations, 94

G

game is over. *See* checkmate
grandmaster status, 26
Greco, Gioachino, 113

H

history of chess
    development, 25
    future, 25
    present status, 25

I

information
    checkmate, 15
    focing a draw, 15
    pins and forks, 15
    stalemates, 15
    world chess leaders, 15

K

Kann, Marcus, 114
Kasparov, Garry, 110
king, 24, 68
    attacking piece, 79
    black king, 69
    capture, 79
    movements, 69
    tallest piece on the chessboard, 24
    value, 68
    white king, 69
king (history)
    represented an Indian emperor, 68
knight, 23, 39, 40
    movements, 40, 42
    two dark-colored knights, 39
    two white knights, 39
knight (history)

mounted warrior, 39
professional soldier, 39

L

L-shaped pattern. *See* knight
    movements

M

middle-game advantages, 118
Murphy, Paul, 26

O

objectives
    analyze and develop tactical
        strategies, 17
    define chess terms, 17
    demonstrate chess piece movement,
        17
    explain historical development, 17
    identify and solve chessboard
        scenarios, 17
    identify chess piece, 17
    identify past and present world
        champions, 17
    identify places where chess is
        popular, 17
    visualize positional advantages, 17
opening moves
    Caro-Kann Defence, 114
    English opening, 113
    French Defence, 115
    Giuoco Piano, 111
    King's Gambit, 116
    Ruy Lopez, 110
    Sicilian Defence, 112

P

pawn, 22
    capture, 32, 33
    eight dark pawns, 30
    eight white pawns, 30

foot soldiers, 29
movements, 30, 31, 33, 35, 37
promotion, 37
promotional pawn, 31
value, 30
pawn (history)
    one agricultural worker, 30
    one businessman, 30
    one doctor, 30
    one farrier, 30
    one gambler, 30
    one policeman, 30
    one weaver, 30
    representation of citizens in the
        Middle Ages, 30
pawn (promotion)
    to bishops, 30
    to knights, 30
    to queens, 30
    to rooks, 30
pawn value, 29, 37
Polerio, Giulio, 113, 116
promotion. *See* also queening

Q

queen, 23, 60
    black queen, 64
    capture, 62
    movements, 61, 63
    represents a woman, 60
    value, 61
    white queen, 64
queen (history)
    closest advisor to the king, 60
    fifteenth-century women held
        leadership and influential
        position in their societies, 61
queen characteristics
    powerful, 61
    protective, 61
    quite mobile, 61
    swift, 61
    vicious, 61

wise, 61

queening. *See* promotion to queens

R

ratings, 25

record a game, 93

rokh. *See* rook history, Persian chariots

rook, 22, 53

  capture, 53

  castles, 54

  movements, 54, 56

  progressive attacks, 53

  value, 53, 57

rook (history)

  Persian chariots, 53

rocca (fortified tower), 54

rules of chess

  white pieces *must play first,* 86

S

single overworked chess piece. *See* overload under chess tactics

Spanish opening. *See* opening moves,Ruy Lopez

stalemate, 105, 108

Staunton, Howard, 113

T

three-move repetition, 161

titles

  Grandmasters, 25

  International Masters, 25

  Masters, 25

trap the king. *See* corner the king

U

underpromotion. *See* promotion to rooks, knights, and bishops

W

Western chess, 25

winning strategy, 121

World Chess Champion, 26

  Alekhine, Alexander, 26, 255, 256

  Anand, Viswanathan, 26, 262

  Botvinnik, Mikhail, 256, 257, 258

  Capablanca, Jose Raul, 255

  Euwe, Machgielis, 26, 256

  Fischer, Robert J., 110, 259

  Karpov, Anatoly, 26, 260

  Kasparov, Garry, 260

  Kramnik, Vladimir, 261

  Lasker, Emanuel, 255

  Petrosian, Tigran, 258

  Smyslov, Vasily, 257

  Spassky, Boris, 258

  Steinitz, William, 254

  Tal, Mikhail, 26, 257

X

xiangqi (Chinese version of chess), 25

LaVergne, TN USA
21 March 2010

176620LV00002B/9/P